How To Deal With Your Mother-in-law

How To Deal With Your Mother-in-law

◆

(Sisters & Family Included)

Dr. Bree Allinson

iUniverse, Inc.

New York Lincoln Shanghai

How To Deal With Your Mother-in-law
(Sisters & Family Included)

iUniverse, Inc.

For information address:
iUniverse, Inc.
2021 Pine Lake Road, Suite 100
Lincoln, NE 68512
www.iuniverse.com

ISBN: 0-595-32666-8

Printed in the United States of America

This book is dedicated to all those women who have been hurt by their in-laws. Many of you will never tell your story for fear of the consequences. May this book heal your wounds and give you strength and a positive attitude. For all who shared their stories with me, I hope your stories are able to heal others. To my wonderful daughter, I thank you for all the happiness you have given me. To my darling husband, I'm glad I married you. You have been the best and the worst thing in my life. Thank you for giving me such a beautiful child. I hope you both know how much I love you! To my family, no matter how crazy I am you are always there for me. Thank you for that! Thank you Auntie J for your help and thanks for pushing me to finish this book. To my Mother, thank you for teaching me, and loving me, (oh and walking with me and being my psychologist). To my Nanna I am sorry you were one of the first in our family to be cursed with a hurtful mother-in-law.

Contents

Introduction

There have been many women over the years that have come to me with their personal struggles in dealing with disastrous in-laws and I in turn have shared many of my own stories with them. Eventually, so many women were coming to me for advice on this specific topic that I earned the nickname "Dr. Bree." I struggled myself for a very long time with my own in-laws, but was eventually able to overcome the insecurity of feeling like a terrible wife and mother, and the pain and betrayal I felt when my own husband would side with his family. I gained strength and confidence in finding out that there were other women in the world dealing with the same anxieties stemming from difficult relationships with in-laws, including my own mother! The hurtful details of a poor relationship with mothers-in-law, or any in-law for that matter, are an age-old story that has been kept secret for many years. Women are too afraid of speaking out, in fear that they will make an already bad situation worse. Well, now those of us that have been hurt are speaking out! This book has my personal advice on how to deal with the pain of a hurtful in-law, polls tallied from interviewing over one hundred women regarding some of the common questions which arise when there exists a poor relationship with an in-law, and I have also included true stories I collected from the same women about their personal dilemmas with their in-laws. In combining all of this information some common signs arise on how to spot a bad situation and run, what you should know before you go any further in your relationship, and finally, how to be the #1 woman in your mans life. Last but not least, chapter upon chapter on how to deal with your new family, especially the matriarch, a.k.a. *the mother-in-law.*

There are few books out there on this subject. The people who do write them use the psychobabble they learned in their college psychology class, which most normal people don't understand. This book is written in all laymen's terms; it's easy for all to read.

The next thing I want to point out is that a lot of people write books that claim in the title that it will help people with difficult mothers-in-law's, but in the end turns out to describe how sweet their mothers-in-law are. (Those people wrote their books and showed them to their mothers-in-law to score some points, which isn't a bad idea!) This book isn't designed to criticize in-laws. Some people are blessed with wonderful in-laws therefore I must state that obviously many things that are said in the pages to follow do not apply to the majority of all in-laws. My hope in collecting these stories is simply to show those women who do struggle with their mother-in-law that they are not alone and that their situations are common within a certain group of women.

The stories in this book are true and many are mine, but the names of the women have been changed to protect their identities. They come from generations of all types of women, from all over, with difficult in-law situations. I pray this book will help you in your time of need.

How it starts

◆

Part 1: The Beginning

Let us set the stage with the setting of a brand new relationship! In the beginning everything always seems wonderful. You fall in love; you have the nervous little butterflies in your stomach. This man is amazing. Eventually, after several dates he tells you he wants you to meet his family. Oh wow! You are honored to do this.

"He truly loves me," you say to yourself.

So the date is set, you will be spending this Thanksgiving with his entire family. You are very nervous, but so excited that you are serious enough with your new boyfriend to be introduced to the inner circle of his family!

Today's the day. You did your hair, makeup, and are dressed your cutest. You arrive at the house and the first person you meet is your boyfriend's father. He's a cute old man, and he looks like your own guy. He winks at his son telling him, "Wow, what a catch!" You feel great (maybe I could stay in this family).

That's one down, but there are still many family members to go. His sisters run past you screaming and shouting. They give you the once over and continue on their way. They are a bit loud for your taste but not a big problem. Then you round the corner and there she is, the Queen Bee.

"Mom this is the girl I've been telling you about." Your boyfriend says.

Okay, here is a quick piece of advice, at this point, *kiss up!* Be as charming as you can and immediately say, "Its so nice to meet you, you have a lovely home" Even if she hates you from the first glance everyone will think you are very well mannered and polite.

This first meeting can go many ways:

- Your boyfriend may introduce you as his friend "so and so". His mother might love you. She thinks that the two of you are not serious and there is no threat. She loves that her little boy has friends.

- She may give you the evil eye and say that she has to set the table but it was nice meeting you. This scenario is short and not too sweet.

-     She might make a huge stink about you in front of the entire family and shout, "You are gorgeous!" "I just love your outfit!" "What a beautiful face!"

She could be doing this as an act or like I said, she is truly nice. We shall see. No matter how it went you never paid attention or cared to think about the signs because you were in a blinded by love and only thinking about your new boyfriend. But down the line you will remember small signs from the beginning and think, "Oh wow, I forgot she did that!"

But, I love her…

Here are a few very common lines from women in the first month or so of a relationship:

"His mom loves me, we go shopping, out to lunch, and she buys me all kinds of things."

"We are like girl friends, we always talk on the phone."

"She is so nice, I like her better then my own mother!"

"We get along fine enough, we just kind of stay out of each others way. When we are together she seems sweet enough."

This one is what I hear the most though:

"She loves me more than him."

Okay, the woman may act like she loves you now, but she in no way loves you more than her own son. She barely knows you! These women always end up asking me how they could have been so wrong. I always tell them all the same thing, that it isn't that they were wrong it is that in the beginning it is hard to notice the signs that a potential mother-in-law hates you! A person can't be expected to be looking for danger signs when they are head over heals in love. Love distracts us.

Let the games begin

Let's continue with our new relationship scenario. You have met the family and after a few months of dating you are now a bit more serious. The mother realizes you are now boyfriend and girlfriend. You are now introduced as:

"This is my girlfriend so and so."

If his mother is the dangerous type she sees that you two are getting serious and starts to worry more than before. She is thinking she must do something!

"When my boyfriend told his family that we were officially engaged his mother said we couldn't date because I was from a Lutheran background and he was raised Catholic. His mother said it so fast that I think she was just so flustered by the moment that she just blurted out anything she could to disagree with the idea that we were engaged."

Brianna, Age 24

"When we first declared we were an item my man's mom called up one of his old female friends that my boyfriend used to have a crush on. His mother asked the girl and her mother over for lunch. They all talked for hours about this girl's year abroad and the "good old days". Then my boyfriend's mom actually set up a dinner date for him with this girl! This all happened while I was at work and his mom didn't know I was getting off early that night. I got to the house with no clue what had happened. My boyfriend was all dressed up and shaven. His sister came in the room and said to me in a tone that would make anyone furious, "Amy said she wouldn't go out with him unless he got dressed up and shaved."

I was furious! I looked at my boyfriend and said, "You're going on a date?"

He said, "You are going too, you're my girlfriend."

"I was still mad this had to happen at all. His mom didn't know I was going but was still glad that there would at least be a chance that the other girl would steal him away from me. She never did though! Ha!"

Rita, Age 30

"My boyfriends mom would always call and visit his ex-girlfriend and tell her how my boyfriend was doing."

Isabelle, Age 23

"After my boyfriend and I had been together for two and a half months, his mom sent him to Europe. She told him she would pay for everything if he wanted to go. Of course he wanted to go if she was paying for everything so he told her he yes. She bought his tickets and planned the trip to last three and a half months. He had only wanted to go for a month. He asked his mom why she had made the trip so long."

Her answer was, "Any shorter and you won't get to experience everything."

"The truth was she was hoping we would forget about each other. But unfortunately for her it made our relationship much stronger. We eventually got married and my husband still says to this day that his trip was what made him realize he couldn't live with out me."

Tina, Age 38

"My mother-in-law used to call me my husbands ex-girlfriend's name all the time when we first started dating. She knew the names were totally different. My name is Tatum and hers was Amy. She even wrote his ex's name on a few of my birthday and thank you cards. I wish she would respect me a little more than that."

Tatum, Age 29

"My boyfriend had to take a business trip for a few weeks. His mother and I dropped him off at the airport a few hours away. On the ride home she was asking me about my past relationships. I told her about how my ex-boyfriend had been a spoiled, rich, momma's boy."

All of the sudden my boyfriend's mom freaked out and screamed, "*Well, Gavin isn't a momma's boy is he!*"

"Good Lord! I barely knew this woman. She seemed like such a nice, quiet person. I guess I would have to say that was a big danger sign. In retrospect, I shouldn't have said that in the first place, because Gavin isn't a momma's boy, but his mother wishes he were. I should have avoided the term all together!"

Jamie, Age 33

"When my husband and I first got together his mom loved me. She always spoke highly of me to the family, but once she saw that her son was falling in love with me, she turned on me. She started telling all her friends that he didn't like me and we weren't dating anymore. Then, on top of lying about us breaking up, every time, I called for him she would say he wasn't home. Or, if he weren't there she would pretend to take a message and I know that she never once gave him the message that I had called. I kept track she never told him."

Eve, Age 26

"My mother-in-law had my husband (who was my boyfriend at the time) go to the prom with another girl. She made him go with her friend's daughter who didn't have a date because she had missed a bunch of school because she caught mono. At the time he wasn't man enough to say that he was going to the prom with me because he knew his mom hated me. We weren't that serious yet, but she didn't have to ruin my prom! It was my senior prom and this other girl's junior prom. So she had another year and I didn't. After 10 years of marriage I still get sick over this story."

Rose, Age 32

Most of these stories are the first signs of an imminent dysfunctional power struggle between you and your mother-in-law. For the most part the mother will pull these stunts behind your back, i.e. making your man do things that would possibly damage your relationship or flat out slip up and yell at you. A son is usually blind to the things his mom does because he thinks he knows her. The mother on the other hand has never had her position threatened before. She has had her son's love all to herself his entire life until you came around. If he had another serious girlfriend before you the mother may be a bit more broken in, but nevertheless if she is jealous and threatened, she is going to be very damaging to your relationship with her son.

Many women I have met with said the few years their boyfriends and their boyfriend's mothers didn't get along were the years they had serious girlfriends. That in itself is a *huge* clue! If there is a history of the Queen Bee acting up when her throne is in jeopardy you better get ready for a fight.

Run, Run, Run...

When you encounter signs like these, you should be afraid. You are going to need your man to be yours not his mothers.

"Even after we had been together five months, his mother still called my boyfriend at least ten times a day on his cell phone. I'm not joking, every time she knew we were out together she would find something to call and talk to him about."

Uma, Age 28

"I should have known she was a problem when she started putting books in the bathroom titled, 'Mom' or 'Why I love My Mom,' and none of her sons read them."

Brietta, Age 21

"I dated this guy whose mother actually came to me and set me up with her son. After two months of us dating she broke it up. Then she moved on to another girl. She didn't want her son to date anyone longer than a few months, so that he wouldn't get too attached I know that eventually he would be unable to commit altogether! Watch out for the controlling ones!"

Rhonda, Age 26

"Unfortunately my boyfriend is a momma's boy. We go to college together in New Jersey and we both live on campus. His mother, father, and sisters live in Florida. After September 11th happened he was not at school and no one knew where he was. He always called me so I thought he was hurt in New York or something. Days went by without a single call. I finally saw him again at school and asked where he had been all week. He told me he went home to protect his mother and sisters. I was closer to the action and was his damn girlfriend what about saving me!"

Ingrid, Age 19

"When my husband and I first started dating I called him once and his mom answered the phone."

I said, "Oh, hi it's Jerusha, Geoff's girlfriend."

She answered, "Hi Jerusha, this is Geoff's number one girlfriend."

"I should have seen through the sarcasm and run away!"

Jerusha, Age 31

"My husband has always said that his mom is his best friend. They are very close and do everything together. She acts like his girlfriend and she never lets me have much time alone with him. I want to be his best friend."

Tonya, Age 27

This one was important to me because many guys are momma's boys and don't admit it, this particular guy did admit his mom was his best friend and Tonya loved her husband in spite of it, but she should have also known what she was getting into. Some people can be quite happy as #2. I for one would not be.

I sat down with the couple and asked the husband if his mother was always going to be his best friend.

He replied, "She and I will always be close and I can't imagine her not being my best friend."

I told him to have a healthy relationship in the future with his wife he can have his mom close but his wife needs to be his best friend and have priority over his mother. Women can have closer relationships with their mothers, but the mother should never stand in the way of being best friends with your spouse. Men must form this same bond with their father or another male figure. If the wife is not #1 there will be serious problems in the future.

"My fiancé's mother called him on our first year anniversary when we were out to dinner at a fancy restaurant. She told him her sink was broken and it needed to be fixed immediately. She said that so much water was pouring out the house was flooding and the water wouldn't stop. The sad thing is that instead of calling a plumber for her, he left me and fixed it himself. The flood turned out to be a leaky faucet. I can't wait for what's in store for us after we are married."

Tina, Age 32

It is sad to say but many men are momma's boys. We have to face the issues if we choose to love our men in spite of them being too attached to their mothers. We can do something about the future and fight back. There will be more stories and advice on how to deal with a momma's boy as you read further into the book.

As for the signs, try to notice if he is too big of a momma's boy from the start, and he is saying his mom is his best friend. Another obvious sign is that his mom doesn't like you at all. Take these two signs into consideration early on. You might want to get yourself out of the picture. The choice to stay is yours if you don't mind these things and your boyfriend's mom seems okay. If there are a lot of signs that she hates you she might make your life a living hell. Trust me I've seen it.

Let's Review

- When you first meet your boyfriend's mother or any of your potential in-laws, kiss up, smile, and compliment. They most likely already hate you but your man and others will see how nice of a girl you are.

- In the beginning you might like your boyfriends mom, but keep watching for signs that she is a crazy psycho!

- Your guy is not going to know what you're talking about if you tell him his mom yelled at you or did something in a spiteful way. He has known his mother his entire life and she has never done anything of that nature before, so he won't understand, unless of course he dated another girl seriously and already went through a similar situation.

- If your man listens to his mom over you all the time and says she is his best friend, *run!* It will only get worse. Many of you reading this are far past this point but there is still a lot of advice for you to help you take control of the situation and be #1! I have to at least try to save a few newcomers from suffering as much as we have!

Part 1 Poll

The following polls were taken by 100 women ranging across 3 different sections of the United States regarding a series of questions I asked them about their relationships with their families-in-law. These women come from all walks of life—Different ages, cultures, religion, race, and creed.

-   **60%** Said their mothers-in-law were nice in the beginning, and then changed slightly once the relationship became serious.

-   **42%** Said they paid no attention to the obvious signs of the mother's hatred and jealousy towards them in the beginning of their relationship.

-   **65%** Said the mother changed drastically for the worse when she knew the two of you were serious.

-   **70%** Said that your man had no idea that his mother's behavior was spiteful and directed towards you, even if she said things to you in front of him.

-   **30%** Said they knew their man was a momma's boy when they first started dating.

Things Get Worse

◆

Part 2: Engagement

Okay, the setting of our relationship is no longer new. The two of you are now engaged. Things were bad when you were seriously dating and his mother knew he was in love with you. Now he has told everyone that the two of you are engaged. You have the ring and the date set for the big day.

"The day after we got the engagement ring my fiancé's mom showed me an old photo album she had made for my fiancé. It had pictures of all his old girl-friends."

His mother just kept going on and on, "This was Scott's old girlfriend Jessica, she was the nicest girl." And "Oh, there they are again at Disneyland, isn't she so pretty, look at those eyes." Then she said, "I need to finish this and give it to Scott."

"Why on earth would she do that?"

Amy, Age 25

"My mother-in-law gave me a speech before I was married about whose fault it was if my boyfriend and I had sex! She said if we did have sex then it would be entirely my fault even if her son were the one who wanted it, because I am sup-posed to be the one in charge. It's the girl's choice to be the rock. It wouldn't have been so bad if she said it sincerely and with honest concern for me, but she said it with anger and accusation."

Nancy, Age 22

"My fiancé's mom always put together family gatherings at her house. She would call and invite everyone and tell them to bring their boyfriends and girl-friends. My fiancé still lived at home at the time and his mother would plan the parties without telling him so that he wouldn't know to invite me. She wanted her little baby all to her self without the ball and chain. When he figured out the family was coming over he would always call me and I would rush over. I always ended up being the life of the party. It made her mad every time."

Yolanda, Age 25

"My fiancés family and I all went to my fiancés second cousin's wedding. Unfortunately, my fiancé's ex-girlfriend was a friend of his second cousin. When we were at the church, before the ceremony, we met up with my fiancé's ex. His mom asked her to sit with us. We were about to sit down when his mom asked me to help her get something out of the car. I was on to her, but I didn't know how to say no, so I went with her. My man was just sitting there with his ex! When we were on our way back into the church she rushed in front of me and sat next to my fiancé. So I had to sit on the very end next to his mom through the entire ceremony and my fiancé sat between his mommy and his ex. As if that weren't bad enough my fiancé's mother asked me to take pictures of her and my fiancé's ex. I have hated my mother-in-law ever since. My husband and I are married now and she still does stuff like that."

Jessica, Age 28

"One day my fiancé's mom and I went grocery shopping together and a friend of hers came up to us and asked if I was her daughter. She quickly answered, *"Hell No!"*

Emily, Age 22

Planning the wedding

"When we got engaged my fiancé's mom went crazy. She saw us alone talking about wedding plans and she started slamming cupboards and drawers. My fiancé said he didn't know what she was so mad about. I did."

Rachel, Age 35

"I am a very shy person and my mother-in-law is outgoing and overbearing. From the first day my fiancé and I announced we were engaged his mother started planning her, I mean my, wedding. She picked out my colors, the band, everything. We ended up eloping! It saved my life and my nerves."

Una, Age 28

When planning a wedding it's important to plan your day the way you want! It's *your* day and it is only going to happen once! You can let your mother-in-law go with you to pick things out, but make sure she knows which things you like best. If you are shy or non-confrontational and don't want to create waves with her here are a few helpful tips:

Ask your family or friends if you can use them as an excuse as to why things need to be done a certain way. For example:

> "Well the swing band sounds great but my mom's good friend is a DJ and he will do it for next to nothing. I don't want to hurt his feelings."

> "My best friend picked out the dresses for me and she is never going to get married so I thought I could let her be a big part of the wedding."

Always follow up with something like:

> "It's too bad they can't be stronger and more secure with themselves like you are. They are very needy."

If your mother-in-law is that self-centered most likely flattering her ego will make her ease up a little bit, but I'm sure she will still try to push stuff on you. Keep enforcing what you want or "your friend wants". It is a bizarre thing that she can hate you so much but at the same time want to control the wedding that will tie you forever to her son.

The best and most important way I suggest you handle your in-laws is to have your husband deal with his family! The number one thing in dealing with his family is having him do it. (That should have been the title for this book!) It is his family and he knows how best to deal with them. If it is something that makes them mad they will most likely forgive him sooner than you. The same goes for you. If a problem occurs with your family, you must deal with it. If you learn anything from this book I hope it is this!

The Big Day

✦

Part 3: Letting Go or Holding Tighter

This is it! The big day! A time for celebration, you and your husband have become a new family. People will be telling your new mother-in-law how great it is that she has gained a daughter. In her mind the wedding is not a day of happiness it's an eye opener to her that she is losing her son. With this in mind she is very moody during the wedding planning and especially the day of the wedding. She is so jealous; this day is all about you and *her* baby.

"At the reception the first dance is the bride and groom dance, you know, when the bride and groom share the spotlight and get the party started. That's what we had planned at least. Well, my mother-in-law talked to the DJ the day before and made the mother-son dance first! Thank God for the champagne in the limousine!"

Sara, Age 30

Try to feel sorry for your mother-in-law, she is so jealous and she has lost her son. She had him in the beginning and you get him for the rest of your lives (or in Sara's case the rest of the reception.)

"During the wedding ceremony, as we were saying our vows, my mother-in-law started wailing and crying at the top of her lungs. I have never heard her do anything like that before. She didn't even do this at her own daughter's wedding. Everyone was talking about it afterward and how it ruined the wedding! I later watched our video and you can't even hear us. All you can hear is the banshee!"

Hailey, Age 34

"I was so excited after we finally got married. Finally after all the months of planning, and not to mention all the money we spent on the wedding, we were married! Anyway, at the last minute a few of my mother-in-laws friend's couldn't make it so she took it upon herself to invite other people. I didn't see them until we were going from table to table greeting the guests. There is my new mother-in-law sitting with my husband's ex-girlfriend. Then, after we said our hellos and were walking away I heard my mother-in-law telling this girl how she wished her son had married her instead of me! I just about passed out."

Abby, Age 25

"When I got married, my mother-in-law showed up three hours late to the wedding. She only lived forty-five minutes away and there was no traffic. Everyone thought she was hurt or something. She finally came waltzing in and said to my husband that she was late because she had to run some errands and get her hair done. She just wants as much focus on her as she can get."

Heidi, Age 40

"When my husband and I got married we had a small wedding but it was still pretty classy. When the pastor asked if anyone had any objections to the marriage his mom jokingly got up and said she objected!"

She sat down and said, "I'm just kidding." (She most likely was *not* kidding.)

Eileen, Age 36

"My mother-in-law actually kept a bunch of my bridal shower gifts. The only reason I know this is because two of my cousins and one of my girlfriends asked how I liked my gifts:

- A bunch of lingerie.

- Sexy pajamas

- A pair of earrings that my mother-in-law was wearing at the wedding.

The person who gave me the earrings also gave me the lingerie so I know it wasn't misplaced. I hope my mother-in-law doesn't wear my lingerie."

Danielle, Age 23

Home At Last

◆

Part 4: It's Only Just Begun!

Okay, now the wedding is over and you have returned from your honeymoon so, get ready! (If your mother-in-law is as crazy as most of the women's mothers I have talked to she most likely called you the entire time you were on your honeymoon!) You are feeling rested and excited to be home, settled, and finished with everything. Be prepared because, now, is the worst time of all. The mother-in-law will want her son back more then ever!

The reason for this is simple. It is because he won't need her as much. It's also very hard if your husband went from living at home with his parents to living with you because his mother won't get to see him as often. This all keeps making a dysfunctional mother-in-law more and more jealous, and that delusion makes her fight to be back in the number one slot.

"My mother-in-law called constantly, (at least ten times a day.) If I answered she would just ask for my husband."

She would ask him things like, "Would you like me to make you some dinner?" or "Do you want anything at the store?" and "Can I buy you anything?"

"She never asked me once!"

Irene, Age 27

"One night my husband stubbed his toe and it got completely black and blue. His mom called to say goodnight to him (not me) and he explained how he hurt his toe. She said she would be right over to give him this cream to help the swelling. It was 11:30pm at night and she lived an hour away. I just told him to put some damn ice on the thing. The woman actually came all the way over and proceeded to rub the stupid cream all over my husbands toe like he was a little kid!"

Becky, Age 32

"My husband and I had just finished visiting my mother-in-law all day and I now had to go to work. We had a nice lunch and I told her how I loved my new job and how I had to go to work that night. She asked if we took two cars so that my husband Anthony could stay a bit longer. We explained that we took one car and had to leave together."

So she said, "Oh, okay," with a bit of a pout and went to do the dishes.

"Then after she was done with the dishes she excused herself to the bathroom. I had to get to work, but I waited for a while. I walked passed the bathroom to tell her I had to leave and saw that the door was open so I looked closer and there she was trying to break the head off the shower! She eventually succeeded, and of course she then came out and asked my husband to fix it. She told me she would drive him home."

Raquel, Age 35

"A few weeks after my husband and I got married, his ex-girlfriend, with whom he had dated pretty seriously, wanted him back and was writing him love letters. She was sending the letters to his parent's address because she didn't have ours. His mom of course sent them to us because she knew it would create problems. After he got one of the letters he told his mom not to forward them and to throw anything from her away. She told my husband that she wasn't going to do that and that I would just have to grow up. She kept sending the letters to us. My husband never read any of them anyway, but still, my mother-in-law has no respect for my feelings."

Ivy, Age 24

"When my new mother-in-law and I got together to go to lunch she told me that she didn't want me to call her mom. She said she preferred I call her by her first name. I was only insulted because I had never tried to call her mom. I had always called her by her first name. She was basically telling me that just to hurt me."

Tamie, Age 20

"My mother-in-law said she wanted to be called mom by all her son/daughter-in-laws. I feel weird calling her mom because she was always so mean to me. I had been calling her by her first name for five years before my husband and I even got married. That is what I was used to. Now I don't call her anything."

Monique, Age 35

"The day my husband and I got married my mother-in-law suddenly started calling my husband by his full name, Jonathan. She had been calling him John or Johnny his entire life! I think it was some strange attempt to show me that he is still her baby, and is the one that gave him his name. I couldn't tell you the reasoning behind it, just that it was directed at me."

Tamiko, Age 28

"One time, soon after my wedding, I was at home organizing all my wedding gifts and putting them where they needed to go. My mother-in-law decided to come over that same day. She let herself in and saw me putting away the pots and pans I had received."

She said, "You know dear I will take those off your hands, because Lord knows you won't ever be cooking."

"I just looked at her."

Then I said, "Actually, I will be keeping them, thanks though." I tried to make a joke after that to hide my resentment at her comment and said, "I'm going to learn how to cook one of these days."

She started laughing and said, "Whatever you say dear," as she walked out the door.

Yvonne, Age 37

"My new mother-in-law was so desperate to stay close to my husband after he left that she asked him to work with her, even though she knew he was making a lot of money with his current job. (Which, by the way, I helped him get.) Her job was some harebrained scheme she thought was going to make her a lot of money. It was basically one of those scams where you are working your ass off for someone else and never make all that much money for yourself. My husband of course didn't believe me because his mom was so passionate about this idea. He told her he couldn't go in on it with her, but told her she should ask me if I wanted to go in on the idea with her. She told him she only wanted him to do it. Exactly one year went by and she made no money. So, she called my husband up and asked if she could work with him at his job. I would understand her doing this if she needed money but she doesn't, she just wants to be closer to him than me. It's been a long time too, we have been married 15 years and she still can't let go."

Jessica, Age 48

"My husband's mother is so screwed up that she doesn't want any of her kids to leave the nest and get married. She tries to sabotage all their relationships. She actually got two of her kids to get divorces. She meddles in the relationships when there is a fight and tries her best to stop her son or daughter from getting back together with their spouse. So of course when my husband and I got into a huge fight she was right there waiting!"

"The fight was insignificant but I had told him to leave, and he did, but unfortunately he went to his mom's house. After a few days went by he didn't call like he usually does after we fight. I was afraid of what his mom might be saying, so I called the house and his mom answered the phone. When she heard that it was me she said never to call again. I called back and told her to please let me talk to my husband."

"My son doesn't want you anymore I will be sending you the divorce papers!" She snapped.

"Now I was afraid. I knew we loved each other and we had only been together less then a year so we were still just working on being married. We had to try and work it out. I called back once again begging his mother to put him on the phone. I told her if she ever had problems with her husband I would do anything I could to help their marriage. She again told me not to call and hung up the phone. I felt so helpless. I drove to her house and waited at the end of her street for her to leave. She eventually did leave and I drove up to the house and knocked on the door. My husband came to the door and we talked. We forgave each other and he went inside to get his things. Just like a bad movie she turned around and came home. She got out of the car and started screaming at me. She said she had a psychic feeling that her son was in trouble and she had to turn around. She said I was evil and I had to keep my evil away from her son. She called me all kinds of things and then my husband came out and broke it up. He told her he was going home with me. She started crying and trying to grab his shirt, but he just walked away. Thank God! As we drove away she just sat there crying. I have never asked him to leave again."

Elaine, Age 21

"The first six months after we got married were the worst with his mom. She hated my guts. She asked my husband if they could have a mother son day once a week without me there. She also never invited me anywhere. The worst was when she would tell her son to ask me to stay home once in a while when he comes to visit her. I just figured it was a losing battle and I didn't want to deal with her so I gave her what she wanted, I haven't seen her in five months, and since I don't go over to see her, my husband doesn't go much either. Too bad for her, she made things worse for herself."

Raina, Age 37

"My mom and dad got divorced when I was very young and both re-married. They each had more kids in their new marriages and I felt left out as a kid growing up. When I was engaged to my husband I thought it would be great to have a nice family with two parents that had stayed together for so many years. I was excited to be a part of that. When my husband and I were married my mother-in-law told me that she could never be like a real mother to me and that no one would think of me as a part of the family. That broke my heart. I swore I would never hurt my daughters-in-law like that when the time came for my son's to get married, and I have a wonderful relationship with them now, and the family I never had growing up."

Ursula, Age 46

Let's Review

- Remember that the mother's position as #1 woman is now in even more jeopardy. Now that you are engaged or married she knows there is less of a chance of him and you breaking up.

- Mother-in-law to be might give you some type of a sex speech. She is doing this for many reasons, but mostly she just wants to make sure her baby isn't having sex. She also doesn't want him to get attached to you if he does have sex with you. So she wants to yell at you and make you feel guilty so you won't have sex.

- If she forgets to call you for a get together she might have honestly forgot. Either way, just show up and put on a happy face and use your sparkling personality to steal the show.

- If you encounter an ex girlfriend, which is very common, you should *Not* start crying or flipping out and feeling bad. If you do the people trying to tear your relationship apart with your boyfriend/husband will have won. This is hard to do, but put on a smile and stand up tall and confident. Most likely she is jealous of you so don't get jealous of her. You've got her man. If your husband can see your confidence he will most likely be even more attracted to you! If you start a fight with him just because you saw his ex-girlfriend, it's not fair to him and he will think you are psycho. Don't say anything to him, jut smile and when you get home call a friend and tell her all about it. Oh, and hit your pillow a few thousand times!

- When you plan your wedding don't let your mother-in-law start making all the decisions, use anyone who will let you use them as an excuse as to why you can't do it her way. Make sure you get their permission first!

- You might want to unplug the phones after you first get married. Your husband's mom will miss him being around (or being single) so she will call all day long. You might want to get another phone number for friends and your family to call.

- Address your new mother-in-law the way *you* feel most comfortable.

- **Always have your husband deal with his family and you deal with yours.**

Parts 2-4 Poll

- **58%** Said things went down hill even more when they announced they were engaged.

- **26%** Actually said their Mothers-in-law gave them some kind of a sex speech.

- **41%** Said there was at least one time their future mothers-in-law "forgot" to tell them or invite them to a get together.

- **23%** Said they know their mothers-in law would have rather had their son marry his ex girlfriend.

- **49%** Have met their husband's ex-girlfriend.

- **63%** Said their mother-in-law was one of the most stressful things about the wedding.

- **37%** Said it's hard to call their mother-in-law "Mom".

The Rest Of The Gang...

◆

Part 5: Getting To Know Everyone Else

Dear old dad…

Okay, lets take a break from *you know who* and think about something else. How about we discuss the rest of the in-laws. Our new daddy-in-law, he is usually the only one you can stand (or so I have observed and have personally experienced). He usually doesn't want to get involved or say anything about anything because he is a man and men are very different from women. Men aren't jealous of women like his wife may be jealous of you. This does not mean however, that he won't act like a whipped puppy that always agrees with his dominatrix.

"My father-in-law is great he always sides with me and has for ten years. He also makes fun of my mother-in-law. I think he knows how childish she acts."

Mia, age 40

"Usually my father-in-law is nice but when his controlling woman takes charge of something he agrees with her every time. I don't feel too bad, she is his wife and I would like it if my husband did that."

Alecia, 25

"My father-in-law is a pervert. My husband and I love to go swimming in his parent's hot tub after we go to the beach. We would spend an hour or so in the hot tub and a few times I would catch a glimpse of his dad looking at us from inside the house. After I left my husbands father said that he couldn't wait to see me in a bathing suit again. Gross!"

Lacey, age 23

"One day I was over at my new in-law's house helping them plant flowers in their back yard. Of course it was my mother-in-law and I doing the work, or I should say her telling me what to do. My father-in-law is very lazy, but he is nice when it counts. Anyhow, she was telling me how I should work out a little more. She said I shouldn't eat as much ice cream as I do. I only eat ice cream at her house because that's the only thing they have in the house that is any good! Her cooking is worse than mine! I was shocked, but I shouldn't have been. She is that type of person."

My father-in-law heard her and he got up from his chair and yelled out the window, "Mary stop being a bitch!"

"The neighbors all heard him too. She shut up for the rest of the day. I'm so glad that someone can stand up to her."

Laurie, Age 25

"I hate going to my in-laws. I feel sick when I have to see them. The only one I can feel somewhat comfortable around is my father-in-law. He is real, not fake like his wife and kids. He says it like it is. He knows all the weird games they play."

Ivah, 45

"My father-in-law always comes over to watch our TV because our TV is a little bigger than his. He never knocks and just waltzes in and helps himself to everything. One morning I came downstairs in my underwear at about 6:00am and he waltzes in through the front door. I'm sorry, but I had to yell at him! I asked him if he could please start knocking. Thank goodness for me he did. I can't get too mad at him though I know all he wants to do is be around us."

Nadine, Age 34

"I feel so bad for my sisters-in-law. My father-in-law is always telling them how fat they are. His sons are just as chubby as the girls, but he tells the boys that men are allowed to be fat but women are not. He makes them run, and swim. He doesn't even let the girls eat meals with the family sometimes! I can't wait for those girls to be old enough to leave for college."

Sabina, Age 30

"My father-in-law watches dirty movies and has dirty magazines all over his house. He also has a terribly foul mouth. I think if he wants to do any of that, he should do it in private. It makes me so uncomfortable and most likely everyone else too."

Olivia, Age 43

"Unfortunately my husband works for his pervert father. One night after work my father-in-law suggested that all his employees go out with him to a topless bar/restaurant. Every one said they wanted to go. My husband looked at me and asked me if it was okay. I was so mad. I told him he knew how I felt the choice was up to him."

He said, "Okay, I will go, but I won't look at anyone."

I thought, "You have got to be kidding me…" I just about barfed…"I will go but I won't look at anyone?" (Yeah, right!)

"I just drove home. I can't believe that he wants to please his father that much."

Naomi, Age 30

"My father-in-law always talks about his old girlfriends from college in front of his wife who he has been married to for twenty five years."

He will say things like, "Christine was the most beautiful girl I have ever dated." or "I wrote a book about Christine."

"I feel so bad for her. She is shy and very skinny, I almost never see her eat."

If he ever talks about her to his kids, he just says to his sons, "Date the pretty girls and marry someone like your mom."

Eliza, Age 27

"I was showing my father-in-law my wedding pictures that I had developed. He was looking at one and in front of my husband, his mom, sisters, and brothers and he said to me, 'You look chubby in these.'"

"I felt so hurt. My eyes started to well up with tears, but I held them back. My husband's family is a lot different then mine, his family is brutally honest. I just felt bad because they were my wedding photos."

Cameron, Age 23

I would like to stop here for a moment and point out something because things like this happen to me with my in-laws all the time and I have had to learn how to deal with people who don't understand how sensitive you are. When something like that happens, and things like this happen all the time so you aren't alone, whether it's a father, sister, or anyone, you can't be thin-skinned. A great way for Cameron to have dealt with that situation would be for her to have been a bit sarcastic. Sarcasm can be one of your best friends if used properly. People don't know if you are joking or serious. Usually you are serious! So this is how that conversation should have gone:

Dad: "You look chubby in these photos."

You: "Well, that's because I am chubby."

This way you are not backing down and being overly sensitive. You also get the last word in so people watching don't say, "Wow I can't believe she let him say that." People will perceive the whole thing as a joke. If you accidentally say it extra mean or snappy then you could end the slip up with, "Just kidding," or "I'm just joking." Only use this kind of humor if you have to. Don't get into the habit of being sarcastic all the time because people will never know when you are serious or joking. It should only be used as a last resort to hide your hurt and not let people get the best of you.

Lets Review

- You most likely will like your father-in-law more then the rest of the in-laws.

- Father-in-laws will usually stay out of arguments because they just don't want to deal with women arguing.

- You can't feel bad when your father-in-law sides with his woman because you would like if your man sided with you!

- If your new father-in-law is a pervert, stay away from bikinis and hot tubs around him.

- If you have a problem with your father-in-law or any in-law you should confront them or have your husband talk to them. If you face the issue head on then you are giving your in-law a chance to change. If you go your entire life with out saying anything you will change nothing.

- Know when to put your foot down. If your father-in-law always sways your husband show your husband that it's his dad or you. You must always be your husband's #1 priority.

- If anyone belittles you then sarcasm is a great last resort. You make the whole thing a joke and people will see you aren't overly sensitive, but are not a doormat either.

Daddy poll

- **60%** Said they like their father-in-law better then their mother-in-law.

- **20%** Said they don't like their mother or father-in-law.

- **45%** Said their father-in-law is a pervert.

- **30%** Said their father-in-law has insulted them more then once.

- **52%** Said their father-in-law stays out of most arguments.

Oh Brother

This section, like the father-in-law section, is much shorter than the complaints from the mother and sisters-in-law sections. Like the father-in-law your brother-in-law will not be as jealous of you because he is a male. They just aren't jealous of women like another female would be. This is not to say that he won't still have his moments of course.

"My brother-in-law is a penny pincher. He brings a calculator to the restaurants we go to, even the cheap places! He calculates to the penny how much everyone owes. One time we didn't have five cents so he said we could just pay him back. So for the next few days he kept reminding us how we owed him a nickel. The worst thing is we have let him borrow money here and there and we never ask for it back."

Kara, Age 30

"My husbands brother always spends the night and eats all of our food. When we go out we always end up paying for him. I wouldn't mind as much if I were rich but we are struggling to make enough for our selves."

Latanya, Age 22

"My brother-in-law is so selfish. When we have to decide on something he always gets what he wants. He is twenty-eight and should know better by now. Well, I guess I can see why every girl he goes out with dumps him."

Hattie, Age 38

"I hate going places with my husband and his brother. My brother-in-law always looks at girls and tells my husband how hot they are right in front of me. The worst is when we go to the beach."

He will say things like, "Wow, look at her! She has great boobs!"

"I get so mad. My husband is pretty good about it, he doesn't stare at girls like my brother-in-law does."

Elisabeth, Age 26

"My husband's brother does all kinds of drugs and always is asking my husband to do them too. I have already told my brother-in-law I don't like him doing that to my husband. He doesn't listen to me. (Or anyone for that matter.) I especially don't like him pressuring my husband because my husband had a hard time giving up drugs."

Sadie, Age 35

"I have a 6'4" thirteen year old brother-in-law. The kid is huge! He also has a slight mental disorder, but still is able to go to school with regular kids. Whenever my husband and I go over to my in-laws my brother-in-law hugs and grabs me very tightly. He also walks around the house with me in a headlock. I feel bad for him because of his disorder, so for a while I never said anything, but one of these days the kid is going to break one of my ribs! I finally told him to be gentle with me. He stopped for the moment, but the next time we were over, he did it again. All I can do is laugh, but it is getting pretty annoying. I told my husband and he finally took care of it."

Samantha, Age 27

"When my husband's brother goes out club and bar hopping with his friends he meets all kinds of trashy girls. The girls always ask for his phone number and he gives them my husbands cell phone number or our house number. Why? Because if his *wife* knew she would be furious! So, I end up answering his calls at all hours of the night. His poor wife!"

Malia, Age 34

"Every time I go on the computer all these porn sites come up. I just want to get my work done! I finally figured out how to get rid of them, but a few days later there they were again. I couldn't understand it. Finally, I figured out that it was my brother-in-law. He looks it up when my kids are running around and I can't pay attention to what he is doing even though every one is home in the middle of the day. I am mad at him for doing that, but I don't know if I should talk to him or if my husband should."

Anna, Age 30

"When my mother-in-law was out for a few hours one night, my brother-in-law asked if I wanted to cook dinner for the family with him. I said that would be fun. So I spiced up the vegetables and made a great salad. He made the steak. Everyone was eating and said they had never tasted anything so good. My mother-in-law came home and everyone told her that I made the side dishes. She grabbed a plate and only ate the steak. She didn't even touch my food. (Believe me she is on no special diet.)"

My brother-in-law saw what she was doing and said, "Yeah mom, you have to try the broccoli it's even better then yours."

"I couldn't believe he said that. I was so proud. My mother-in-law is the type of perfectionist who thinks she is the best at all things domestic and if any other woman tries to step in she will get bent out of shape. That was nice of my brother-in-law to compliment me like that in front of his mother."

Ronnie, Age 45

"I will never forgive my brother-in-law. The night before my husband and I got married my brother-in-law said he wanted to hang out with my husband at his house. He said he just wanted to play pool and watch TV. I said that was fine. My husband and I decided on no sleazy bachelor/bachelorette parties. Anyway, my brother-in-law had all his football buddies over and my husband's other sleazy friend's. They handcuffed my husband to a doorknob and had a bunch of strippers over. I found out early the next morning. I almost didn't marry him. I had a bunch of champagne and told myself it wasn't his fault it was his jerky brother's fault. Still I was so upset that I couldn't completely enjoy my own wedding day!"

Katy, Age 24

Lets Review

- The most important thing to do with your husband is explain to him calmly what your feelings are. If you go after him like you are accusing him of something he will be on the defense and argue with you. Even if you are right to feel a certain way.

  A good response would be:

  "I am sorry but I feel self conscience, jealous, and sad when you and your brother look at girls."

  He will most likely say he is sorry. It is very hard to keep your cool about many situations, but you have to take a break and think before you speak.

  This is how most people (myself included) might want to react.

  "I can't believe you! I saw you staring at that girl! That's so gross. You are the biggest pervert!"

  All this response will do in the end is make your husband or boyfriend defensive and his response will most likely be some kind of oblivious denial like:

  "What girl?" or "No I didn't."

  This will only escalate the fight, which will eventually turn it to a different fight and keep spiraling downward. Most importantly, you will have solved nothing and you won't feel any better. If you explain calmly and you kiss and make up you will forget the incident faster.

- I'm going to say it again. If you want something changed with your husband or boyfriend's family he has to deal with it. If he won't you should deal with it as politely as you can and tell your in-law(s) what you want them to change. If you never address troublesome issues, things will never be different. If you do ask an in-law to change or do something different, and they continue

to do it then tell your husband or boyfriend to talk to his family member again and get the issue resolved.

Brother Poll

- **27%** Said their brother-in-law is the one who introduced their husband or boyfriend to drugs/alcohol.

- **15%** Said their brother-in-law took their husband to a strip club (before or after their marriage)

- **30%** Said their brother-in-law is the only one in the family they like.

- **10%** Said that their brother-in-law takes advantage of them by eating their food and staying over all the time.

Sisters of Satan. I mean this is the section about sisters.

Well, we had to get here eventually, so here we are. Your sisters-in-law will be almost as bad as your mother-in-law if not worse. Personally my sisters-in-law are better then my mother-in-law, but there are those times when the trouble in dealing with them will be equally as difficult! Sister-in-laws tend to be jealous about the small stuff. What you are wearing, and how your makeup looks that day. These are the little things that fuel their fire. The extra mean ones will give you that sarcastic look and then tell you how pretty you look.

"When I first started dating my husband his two sisters came up to me and said, 'Don't expect us to ever be friends because we won't be."

"I knew I was in big trouble from that moment on."

Scarlett, Age 49

"My sister-in-law had such a problem losing her brother to me that she said to him, 'Let's write each other letters all the time but lets not tell her (meaning me).' She even had curtsey nicknames for him. She was twenty-four too. Sad isn't it."

Christine, Age 25

"My husband and I were having our first baby and every time we saw the relatives they would all ask what we wanted to name the baby. Stupidly, I told them."

I said, "If it's a boy we want to name him Jeffery and if it's a girl we want to name her Holly."

"They all loved the names, especially his sisters. We eventually had our first baby boy and named him Jeffery."

"When I got pregnant again they all asked again what I wanted to name the baby.

I said, "If it's a boy he will be Scott and if it's a girl she will be Holly."

"I loved the name Holly, but we had yet another boy and so we named him Scott. We had another baby after Scott and again it was a boy so we named him Mark, but by this point I wanted a little girl to name Holly, and everyone knew this!"

"Finally, my fourth baby was born and she was a girl and what did I name her? Holly, but then there was a problem. One of my sisters-in-law became very fond of the name as well and told everyone she wanted the name Holly for her baby. So my in-laws had the nerve to all tell me that I shouldn't call my baby Holly! Crazy, right? After all the years I had been talking about naming a little girl Holly! The situation just got worse and my mother-in-law told me that she wasn't going to call my daughter Holly. By this point I was sick about it, I started to get heart palpitations and couldn't sleep. I decided to change Holly's name, but nothing was as good as Holly. So I changed it kept the name Holly. My sisters-in-law both had their babies and they were little girls. Of course my one sister-in-law named her daughter Holly too. When my daughter was growing up my sisters and mother-in-law were very mean to my Holly. They wouldn't include her in anything, and they ignored her at Christmas."

One Christmas my mother-in law went up to my five-year-old daughter and said, "It will be easier on me to keep you and the other Holly straight if I call you Holly 2 from now on".

"My daughter Holly was a year and a half older than my niece Holly! I eventually changed my daughters name to Hailey because I couldn't stand that everyone was so rude to my daughter just because her name was Holly."

"Here is a word of advice, never tell anyone what you are naming your children! Or if you do just make up some bad names and don't tell them what you are going to name them."

Olivia, Age 54

"After my husband and I got married I thought I was going to have sisters to hang out with. One day my sisters-in-law and I drove to a wedding shower together and the entire time they were talking about the sisters' day out *they* were going to have. It sounded wonderful, but I was not included in the conversation. I just sat in the back of the car and was quiet."

Tia, Age 23

"I honestly thought my sister-in-law and I could be best friends. We always hung out and told each other secrets. I told her how I tried smoking pot and she told me how she tried it too. She asked me if I had ever had sex before my husband and I told her I had with one other guy. She ended up telling his entire family! His mom was mad at me and asked me about it. I could not believe it!"

Tamara, Age 22

"My sister-in-law is grossly obsessed with my husband. She and him were never close friends. I met her and she seemed a bit jealous. I stayed in her room once and she didn't have many things up, a few pictures of her and her sister, and some other friends. When my husband and I got married her room decor changed. Her room was covered in pictures of her and my husband. Some had me in them but I was cut out of the picture. She always told the relatives in conversations how "*hot*" her brother was if she was showing them pictures."

She would say things like, "I have this hot picture of Jake with his shirt off and his six pack is showing."

"While she is saying this she is touching her stomach explaining. This is her brother does she know this? She is just plain weird!"

Megan, Age 25

"My husband's sister was starting to be my friend. The last time I saw her we had gone shopping at the mall all day, and saw a movie. She spent the night and we stayed up late talking. The next day we went to the beach and surfed. We left each other happy. The next week she barely said, "hi" to me. We don't fight but we aren't friends. I was hoping for a friend like I had those two days. I have no idea why she changed."

Erin, Age 24

"One time while I was still engaged to my husband we got into a fight and I went home depressed. He and I were supposed to go to a wedding together. He felt bad and tried to call me but my phone was out of batteries. So he told his sister that if I should call to tell me to meet him at the wedding. I called a half-hour later and talked to his sister and asked her if she knew where he was. She said she didn't."

I had a weird feeling she was lying. So I kept asking her, "Are you sure? You have no idea?" She kept on lying to me. So I said, "Okay, just have him call me."

"I waited and knew he was at the wedding, but I didn't know where it was at because it was a family friend getting married and I was never told where the wedding was going to be. I called again and asked his sister if she knew where the wedding was. She said she didn't know and she was the only one home and everyone else was at the wedding, everyone but my fiancé. So I waited hours and hours and my fiancé finally called me. He told me he was at the wedding and would leave early to hang out with me. He said he was going home with his sister. I was figuring he meant his other sister. I got to his house and there was his sister, the one I talked to on the phone, all dressed up! She had gone to the wedding!"

I asked her why she lied and she smirked and looked away. I got so mad and said, "I can't believe you could lie like that!"

My fiancé defended her and said, "Hey, don't be mad at her"

"I couldn't believe he didn't take my side, but I was mostly mad at his sister. I don't trust that she will ever be any kind of help to our relationship."

Gina, Age 27

"My sister-in-law wants to get at me in subtle ways. Whenever I have something in my teeth from dinner or lipstick on my teeth she will never tell me. She is a bold person so it isn't like she wants to spare my feelings. She will tell other people their outfit is ugly or something, or when we go out clothes shopping I will ask my sister-in-law what looks better on me and she always tell me that the less flattering outfit looks the best! So, my new thing is to pick the one she says she doesn't like."

Angie, Age 36

"My husband's sister is such a brat. We play poker with the family every once in a while. When we play his sister gets jealous when I win.

One time she said, "You are only good at poker because you are such a good liar."

"She then proceeded to pout for an entire week."

Nadia, Age 32

"Both my sister and mother-in-law are extremely nosy. They always gossip with each other about other relatives. They try to get as much information about my husband and I as they can from what we say or what they hear from someone else. They always ask us certain very intrusive questions. At different times one of them will try to get me alone to ask personal questions that are none of their business."

One time they both asked me at different times, "So how is your financial situation going?" and "I have heard that you and Rick have been getting into little arguments," and last but not least, "How is the marriage going?"

"It is getting annoying!"

Caroline, Age 36

"My sister-in-law hates me. As soon as my husband started to date me she became best friends with his ex-girlfriend. She is even putting the girl in her wedding. So my husband and I always have to see her. My sister-in-law didn't like the girl when my husband was dating her, but now my sister-in-law knows it will make me mad to have my husband's ex-girlfriend around."

Hannah, Age 23

"When my sister-in-law was getting married I was surprised that she asked me to be one of her bridesmaids. She never acted like she liked me much in the past so I thought she was maturing and maybe wanted to be my friend. She had also asked my husband to be a groomsman. I was thinking she just wanted me in it so I could be with my husband, which would be nice for me. Anyhow, the day of the rehearsal came and all the bridesmaids and groomsmen were standing around. I wasn't paying attention to my order until the part at the end when the bridesmaids and groomsmen paired up and were suppose to walk down the isle. I was confused because I wasn't paired up with my husband."

I looked at his sister and asked, "Aren't I going to be paired up with Joe?"

She came up to me, and the rest of the bridal party, and said, "I was thinking that Joe could be paired up with Sara because it looks good from far away when everyone is in the line."

I said, "What?"

Then she followed up her reasoning with, "You know, because she is shorter than you are."

"I couldn't believe it. Her friend Sara was my height. Here is the real reason I am not paired up with my husband, my sister-in-laws friend Sara has been after my husband for a long time. So far she has gotten a nose and a boob job, and continually seems to lose more and more of her clothing every time I see her. If we are all over drinking and playing poker at my in-laws house this girl always seems to show up and is always all over my husband. She even asked if he wanted to have sex with her! Needless to say, I don't like the fact that his sister is pairing him up with this girl, or even that she is here at all!"

Luckily my brother-in-law spoke up and said, "Mimi, what are you talking about Sara and Reese are exactly the same height, just change it!"

She looked at everyone and started to cry, and then she shouted, "Everyone is trying to ruin my wedding!" She turned around and screamed at her brother, "I had it exactly the way I wanted it, just leave it, *it's my wedding!*" Then she ran off in tears.

"I was about ready to say forget it, I didn't need to be in the wedding, but I wasn't sure what to do. My husband agreed that she was being ridiculous. My husband told me that if it bothered me we didn't have to be in the wedding. I felt bad for Mimi, but I also knew she didn't care about me. So I decided to be the bigger person and let her have it the way she wanted. So my husband went down the isle with Sara and danced with Sara for two of the bridal party dances. I felt sick all day…well actually I still feel sick when I think about it!"

Reese, Age 29

"Sorry but my story has to do with my sister-in-law and my mother-in-law acting like bitches. When my husband and I got married we had a condo twenty minutes from the beach in California. My husband told me how his sister and her boyfriend were going to be staying with us while they were visiting. His sister Amanda came with her boyfriend and stayed for five days then said they were going to stay on a houseboat in San Francisco. Amanda ordered us not to tell my mother-in-law. They left without a thanks or a kind smile to me after all I had done for them. A few days went by and I got a call from my mother-in-law. She asked if I had been in contact with my sister-in-law Amanda because she had told my mother-in-law that she was with one of her girlfriends but my mother-in-law didn't believe her. I did what I was told to do by Amanda and said I didn't know anything. The next day when I was at work I got a call from a very angry mother-in-law. I guess my sister-in-law came home and told my mother-in-law everything, how she was with us for five days with her boyfriend then went to San Francisco. Everyone in my office knew my mother and sister-in-law hated me. So they weren't very surprised to hear my mother-in-law shouting at me on the phone! I just thought it was comical so I put her on speakerphone. Everyone in the office was laughing! I think my sister-in-law wanted to get me into trouble. I don't know what to think, they are all crazy!"

India, Age 35

"One day my sister-in-law and I were going to look at model homes because I wanted to move. I had to go to the information center to get a map and a list of the homes for sale. I had my nine month old daughter in the car too so I asked her if she could just stay in the car with her while I ran in. She said that would be fine. I grabbed what I needed and ran out. I was coming back to the car and saw my sister-in-law digging through my purse with both her hands. I opened the car door and sat down and looked at her. She froze. She slowly put the purse back in the back seat where it was before. I was so taken off guard that I didn't know what to say."

I should have said something like, "Did you need something?"

"She never explained herself. I am guessing she was trying to snoop trough my stuff or maybe steal some money. I guess I will never know."

Sandy, Age 32

"My husband is very close in age to his sister so they have always done stuff together. When my husband and I were getting serious she started to date this guy named Ray. I was excited because we all could do stuff together, like going to movies, and trips, dates fun stuff like that. We have always liked this restaurant that turned into a dance club after ten. We always ate there but never got the chance to stay for the dancing. So one night we were eating there late and figured we might as well stay and dance off dinner. We were all dancing when my sister-in-law said she had to go to the restroom for a second. My husband went also. So I was left with Ray on the dance floor. We were dancing when someone bumped into him, pushing him on me. We were squeezed between people but eventually got further apart. We were laughing about it and he wanted to tell me something and the music was so loud that he had to go right up to my ear. He said that it was getting too crowded and we should get off the dance floor. I just nodded my head, agreeing with him. We made our way to our table where it was a bit quieter. I saw my husband coming back and waved to him but I didn't look behind me. All of the sudden I got a tap on my shoulder I turned around to see a fist flying at my face. His sister belted me in the eye. She started screaming at me and everyone was looking!"

She said that she saw the whole thing and started shouting and cussing, "*You are the biggest whore I've ever met!*"

"My husband grabbed her and took her outside. She told my husband *her* story, how her boyfriend and I were holding each other and how her boyfriend had kissed my cheek!"

"I came out holding my black eye. I was so mad! Ray and I asked her what was wrong with her! She told us what she thought she saw."

"Ray laid into her then and told her that she was way off base and didn't know what she saw."

I chimed in with, "Why in the hell would I do that if you guys were coming right back!"

"She still wouldn't back down. Ray said she was crazy and he was sick of her tantrums. He told her she had crossed the line and that he didn't want to see her anymore. I grabbed my husband and went a different direction. We called my family to pick us up. My husband believed me when I told him what happened, but my sister-in-law still hates me to this day."

Tara, Age 28

It seems to me that the main problem with sisters-in-law is that they are typically very close to your age and there is a natural desire to want to be close friends. Even friends go through moments of jealousy and resentment with each other. Friendships are hard enough to build without being related! A woman can find herself doubling the challenges of creating a friendship with a sister-in-law simply because she has more to be jealous about than a mother-in-law. You have not only taken her brother away without family approval, you will find that you are both typically around the same age and are most likely competing in that aspect as well. Just let the relationship develop on it's own and don't be hurt by your sisters-in-law not including you in their inner circle right away. You don't need them to be your best friends.

Sisters Review

- Unfortunately your sister-in-law may be just as jealous of you as her mother is, so watch out!

- In some cases no matter how much you want to be included as one of the family, you are not going to be treated as a real sister.

- Your sister-in-law may be extremely unpredictable in her moods. She is like you and every other woman, she goes through problems, hormone fluxes, or anything else you can think of that would effect her emotions. You might hang out with your sister-in-law on a good day and the two of you will do all kinds of fun things together. Keep in mind that you are just as likely to catch her on a bad day as well, and in that case the scenario is not going to be too sweet!

- Don't give your sister-in-law all your trust because her loyalty lies with *her* family.

Sister Poll

- **26%** Said they have gotten into some type of verbal fight with their sister-in-law.

- **19%** Said they think their sister-in-law has an oddly close relationship with her brothers.

- **30%** Said their sister-in-laws compliments are never sincere.

- **32%** Said they know their sister-in-law will never truly like them.

Back To Mom

✦

Part 6: Things Are Getting Crazy

Unfortunately, here we are again discussing the dysfunctional things our mothers-in-law do. I would like to stop here for a moment and let everyone know that this next story is one of my own! I have come to laugh about this one over the years and I can tell you that making chili has never been more fun than after this incident!

"My husband never likes the food I cook. He likes his food spicy. I make things that are hot enough for most people, but they are not as spicy as he would like. His great grandmother used to make this chili that was extra spicy and his mom had the recipe. I have asked my mother-in-law for the recipe many times, but his mom always says she has to look it up in her book. I know she can make it with out looking at a recipe."

"Anyway, on the fourth of July my sister, my husband and I, all went to my in-laws house for a barbeque. His parents were having a small get together. My mother-in-law served her famous chili. My sister, my husband and I were eating it and I told them that I had tried to get the recipe from my mother-in-law but she always makes an excuse as to why she can't give it to me. My husband told me to ask her again while he was close by so he could witness his mother try to get out of giving me the recipe."

I asked his mom, and she told me what she always told me "I don't know it off hand, but maybe later I will look for the recipe."

"My sister and husband heard her and laughed. My husband knew his mom knew the recipe. I told my husband to go and ask her because I knew she would tell him."

My husband went up to his mom a few hours later and said, "Mom your chili was great what's the recipe again?"

She saw me standing not to far away and was very hesitant. "You, uh, you use garlic, and some people use chili mix."

I interrupted and said, "What do you use?"

My husband said, "Yeah, what do you use?"

"We could see she didn't want us to know her precious secret!"

She replied, "I use chili powder."

"What a sneak! Chili mix and powder are very different. She hates me so much she doesn't even want me to cook her son food he likes! Later that night my husband looked through her recipe box and found the recipe. (Incidentally, later on she took the recipe out of her box and claimed she had lost it. She has no idea we already found it!)"

I thought it would be fun to give all the readers the secret chili recipe! I challenge all women to use this recipe as well as pass it on to their friends in protest of all women who are mistreated by their mother-in-law's! So here you go! This size is for a party, I hope a lot of people use it…tell your friends!

Crazy Lady Chile:

5 pounds coarsely ground heavy beef chuck, round or brisket.
1-1/4 cup Wesson oil or rendered kidney suet.
2 medium onions
5 level teaspoons of Cumin seeds
8 heaping tablespoons of commercial chili powder
3 cloves of garlic
5-15 Chili pods, depending on heat level desired (if pods are not available, use cayenne pepper to taste)
1 teaspoon dried oregano leaves

Crazy Lady Chili Cooking Instructions:

Remove stems, membrane and seeds from chili pods, cover with water and simmer for 30 minutes. Remove pods and blend into paste.

Hold water.

Chop onions.

Crack cumin with rolling in or grind with mortar and pestle.

Brew 1-teaspoon oregano leaves in 1 cup of water

Brown meat in several batches, add black pepper while browning, Brown onions with meat with meat

Remove with slotted spoon and hold.

Combine browned meat, onion and add the following:
cumin, 8 heaping tablespoons of commercial chili powder, 3 cloves garlic (pressed).

Cook ten minutes, using just enough pepper water to keep from burning. Stir constantly. This cooks the spices into the meat.

Add chili paste and half of oregano water.

Cook slowly, adding pepper water as necessary. Add additional oregano to taste, Salt to taste. The meat should tender in around 1-1/2 hours.

Make sure you get chili powder, not a chili mix or ground chili pepper!

Cooking Variations:

Add 1 to 2 cans of tomato sauce 8oz.

Hand cut meat to about the size of a navy bean.
(A lot of contestants now use half chili grind and half hand cut)

Add 2 tablespoons of vinegar 10 minutes before serving.
Use white pepper instead of black pepper

Use Masa flour to thicken (mix flour with cold water and whisk until smooth, then pour in while stirring)

Dr. Bree, Age 35

"Every time I tell my mother-in-law that I don't want to do something she never gets it. For example, one time she tried to get my husband and I to go on a trip with her. We have gone on trips with her before, but it was a time when we didn't have much money."

I said, "That sounds great! But we can't afford it right now."

She said, "Well, I know you have enough money to go so I will start planning it."

"She acts as though she didn't hear what I said. I guess I will have to start yelling and being impolite to get her to listen to me!"

Inga, Age 30

"One time my husband was telling his mother how some friends of ours didn't talk to us as much anymore."

My husband said, "We think it is because they moved two hours away."

Then out of nowhere, she snapped, "They probably don't like you anymore because Eliza got pregnant before you were married!"

"I did get pregnant a few weeks before I got married but we were engaged. Obviously, she is the one with the issue, not our friends!"

Eliza, Age 24

"My mother-in-law, or should I say Alice, found out my husband and I had sex before we were married. She tells everyone that I am the slut in the relationship and that I made her son do everything. Even though she knew he had sex with two other girls and I was a virgin when I met him!"

Stacey, Age 23

Whenever I talk to my mother-in-law she always tells me, "Mike's life was the best when he was living in another town." or "I know my son better than anyone else."

"One time she was on one of her, 'I know him better than anyone trips,' and she actually said, 'I know that he has been the most unhappy he has ever been since you got pregnant and had the baby."

"I told him about it and he laughed and asked if I was joking. He said that these are his happiest moments of his life and he said his mother is sad and jealous. I'm glad he understands but she still gets under my skin!"

Tatum, Age 24

"My husband Derrick and I have been married for five years now. In all that time my mother-in-law has managed to avoid putting up a single photo of me up in her home. She has three other kids and plenty of pictures of friends up on her refrigerator and in frames around the house, but none of me. She has two of my son and plenty of Derrick's. I think she heard me the other day when I was talking about it to one of Derrick's cousins so she dug up two photos of me and put them on the refrigerator. Lets just say I was happier not being on the refrigerator of shame. The pictures were awful! One is of me with bad hair and I am closing my eyes, the other I am talking and making some weird face! The worst is that they were up the day all the relatives were over so everyone saw them! I moved the pictures under other ones to hide my face, but I should have just taken them!"

Miriam, Age 32

"When ever I try to tell my mother-in-law a story or she asks me a question she will never look at me when I am talking and then she will actually just walk away and join someone else's conversation. For example, the other night, she came over and I was telling her how earlier I had passed a crime scene where someone was killed. I wanted to tell her about it. So I started to describe what happened, and the entire time I was talking, she was looking at my husband as he was cleaning his fish tank. When I was about into my second sentence describing how I had just seen my first dead body, she gets up and walks away and asked my husband what he was doing. He was cleaning a fish tank! How riveting is it to watch someone clean algae off of glass! This coming from a woman who can follow a conversation going on in a different room while listening to you!"

Aleiha, Age 46

"Things with my mother-in-law have gotten so ridiculous it's just plain silly, and I just laugh. The thing that bugs me a lot about my mother-in-law is that she always disagrees with everything I say. I'm serious when I say, everything! She especially loves to argue in front of other people. If I say a movie is good or I have an opinion about a news event she will always take the other side."

For example:

Me: "Oh, I just loved that move, the costumes were beautiful!"

Devil mother: "No, no, I didn't care for it much. It was a bit to fake and the costumes needed a ton of work."

"It's not that she likes to be negative, it's only with me that she does this. If she says she believes in the women's right to choose abortion and my husband disagrees and his opinion is that abortion is murder no matter how old the fetus is, she changes her story."

My mother-in-law would come back with, "Oh yeah, that's right it is flat out murder."

"Acting like she believed what he did the entire time and we all misunderstood what she said at first. I guess if she hates me, she hates everything I believe."

Jean, Age 22

"I know it sounds bad but my mother-in-law is so old now that she doesn't scare me anymore. She was awful to me throughout my thirty-two years of marriage. She would always talk about me to people and was rude and mean to me. I finally got up enough courage to ask her why she hated me so much and why for so long."

Her response was, "Well, you, you can't even swallow a pill!"

"The only thing she could come up with after all those years was that I couldn't swallow a pill? So what if I have to crush my vitamins and put them into jelly that's no reason to hate someone! I realized it was nothing I did, she was just so jealous of me and hated me for marrying her son."

Stephanie, Age 57

"I can honestly say that my mother-in-law is a horrible person. She divorced her husband after years and years of marriage because she wanted to, 'meet some hot dudes.' (Her words not mine). She has always hated me, and she has always been very selfish and is terrified of someone outshining her or having a better situation than her. Five years after being divorced my father-in-law was dying of lung cancer. She found out and knew she wouldn't be in his will. He had made it out to his three daughters and his son, (my husband.) She marched off to the hospital one day because she knew he was still in love with her and used that as ammunition. My sister-in-law and I were with him when she barged into his hospital room."

She said, "My sweet husband, I am so sorry." Then she took his hand and said, "I love you, I've made a horrible mistake, and I want to marry you again before you die!"

"He was so excited. Later they were talking, still with us in the room and she told him she would marry him as soon as he changed his will to include her again. She said she thought it would be best if everything went to her. She told him that way none of the kids will fight over the money. He was on such heavy medication that he just agreed with her."

My sister-in-law started to argue with her and my mother-in-law snapped, "I deserve it, I lived with him all those years."

"It started a huge fight, but I stayed out of it. My father-in-law eventually changed the will to the way my mother-in-law wanted it. When they were married again she treated him just as badly as she had before and he died a few weeks later. My husband and I got nothing, but we felt so bad about what she did that we didn't care. I never want to be around her again."

Cecile, Age 54

Is my baby sick? Move over!

"My mother-in-law almost never comes over. In two years she has been over two times. My husband Jake kind of understands how she is. His mother has that sort of mother hen thing going on. My mother-in-law is a nutritional consultant and thinks she knows everything about health. So obviously, when my husband got a bad flu he wanted to ask her for advice. I was very wary of him calling and asking her to help him because once he does that she feels like she can take over. He called her and she wanted to come over to bring some vitamins and things. My husband Jake asked her if I could go meet her somewhere. She kept on insisting on coming over. Like I said, she never comes over when I ask her to. Even for our daughter's birthday or something. We only live twenty-five minutes away. We always have to go to her house. Anyhow, she finally agreed that I could meet her at a halfway point to pick up the vitamins for Jake. She had to have us meet at 5:30pm and it took me twenty-five minutes because of the rush hour traffic. She was waiting there and told me she had been waiting a long time and thanks to me she actually forgot to bring what I was meeting her there for. I figured she would pull something like that. So she told me that she would just come over later that night to bring it. I had to drive back in the traffic. The entire way home I was thinking, "What a waste of time!" When I told my husband what happened he thought it was funny. I was mad about it because I was working hard around the house and I had to take time out of my day for nothing. Then the phone rings and it's her telling Jake she is coming over and is asking for directions. Like I said, we have been here for two years but she would of course need directions because she never comes over. I drank a glass of wine before she came over to help numb the pain of her inevitable arrival and attempted domination! I suddenly felt very nauseous when I heard the doorbell ring."

I opened the door and she walked right passed me to Jake saying, "How's momma's boy feeling?" Then she announced, "I brought all the things you need, and I also bought you some magazines." She then had the nerve to say, "You just need someone who can take care of you."

"I just stood there and smiled. Lord help us if she'd heard my inner dialogue!"

She then stood up to look over the house. She said, "Where did that scuff come from?" as she pointed to a half an inch long white scuff on our coffee table leg.

"I had the house looking nice so she wanted to find any problem with it she could. So I just answered flatly, "I think someone moved a chair next to it and it bumped it." I guess I am glad she doesn't take me up on my offers to come over."

She walked around a bit more then said, "You should move your end table over to the other side of the room it looks awful there." She then continued to talk to my husband and ignore me.

"I would ask her if she wanted anything and she wouldn't respond. I think I am definitely done with seeing her for a while!"

Diana, Age 29

Kids

✦

Part 7: *As Long As They Don't Get Their Grandma's Personality, We Are Okay!*

When you have children your life has changed, you are very happy to experience all the new and wonderful ways to take care of this new family member. Remember though, that there is a certain in-law who will want to rear her ugly head and ruin the experience.

"My husband Paul and I were so excited to have a baby. We had a family baby shower and everyone was there. We couldn't have been happier. That night when everyone had left except my mother-in-law she started asking about the delivery. She wanted to know things like if I wanted anesthetics or not."

She then asked, "Who else will be in the delivery room other then you and Paul?"

"I was so stunned by her question that I couldn't answer for a few seconds. This lady hasn't been the best mother-in-law to say the least."

I finally gathered my wits and said, "I guess, I don't know."

She said, "Maybe it is best that just Paul and I are there."

"I couldn't believe it! She knows how much I love my mother and she didn't even mention her! All I know is my mother-in-law sure isn't invited into the labor room. I will get security on her if I have to!"

Maria, Age 22

"When I was in labor my family and my husband Sean's family were all in the waiting room. My family was talking about the baby. They wondered what color hair and eyes the baby would have. They were thinking about how everything was going and were getting excited about how it would only be a few more hours until they could see the baby. Sean's mom was trying to talk about something else, or rather she was trying to talk about herself."

She said, "When I was in labor I was a lot faster than this," and "I was always the best at guessing the baby's weight," and "I looked so good after I had my baby, I lost all my weight in a week."

She just kept going on and on saying things like, "My children always came out perfect, they had great coloring," and "I just hope Heather can have a decent size baby. She didn't look very big." She went on to explain that, "With my first delivery the doctors and nurses all kept thinking I was the perfect patient, because I knew everything I was supposed to know before they even told me."

"On and on and on she went!"

"After I had the baby everyone came in to the delivery room and couldn't stop talking about the baby. My sisters came up to me and kept asking me if it hurt and how the IV felt."
Of course my mother-in-law started it up again with, "When I had my first baby…"

"My mom came up to me and told me how Sean's mom had been rambling on and on the entire time they were in the waiting room. I thought it was funny and I felt bad for her because she was trying so hard to get attention."

Heather, Age 20

"My mom and dad wanted to have a small party for mine and my husband's new baby. It was just our closest friends and both of our families. We were all having a great time talking and everyone loved seeing the new baby. Everyone was trying to guess who the baby looked like. At this point my mother-in-law was getting totally drunk. My friend Allie said the baby had my nose and ears for sure."

My mom said, "The baby has Charlie's hair color."

That is when my mother-in-law chimes in after far too many drinks and slurs, "Za baby looks nothing like my family! Are you sure za pizza delivery boy isn't za fazzer?"

"Everyone just stood there and it was dead silent. My mother-in-law was not kidding about thinking it wasn't my husband's baby!"

Thank goodness for my brother interrupting and saying, "Hey who wants to play a game of pool?"

"I was so mad and embarrassed! My poor family had invited her over and she ruined the party. From that moment on everyone was uncomfortable around her. I wish I had said something but I didn't want to be rude. I will just have to forget about it and try to stay away from her as much as possible."

Callie, Age 26

"When I first started breast feeding it was hard for me to get the hang of everything so I liked to take my daughter into another room to feed her. My mother-in-law told me that I didn't have to leave the room to feed her. I said thanks but she gets squirmy and takes the blanket off. (I didn't want my father and brothers-in-law to see my boobs!) Later that night I had to feed her again and I started to walk towards the other room."

My mother-in-law was furious and she yelled, "You don't always have to leave! No one cares!"

My husband yelled back at her, "Just let her do what she wants."

"So I went into the living room to feed the baby. I had her under a blanket but like I said she liked to pull at it. My mother-in-law comes huffing and puffing in and sits down next to me."

I thought she was going to apologize or something but I was wrong. She was still mad and said, "No one cares if they see your breasts or not."

I replied, "Well, I don't want your husband and teenage sons seeing my boobs, because they are not always working boobs they are also bikini boobs!"

"That was the only way I knew how to explain it. I could have just been rude and said I didn't want her horny sons, not to mention her husband who loves playboy, looking at my bigger then normal breasts! My mother-in-law was just sitting there and I hadn't realized that I had a small slit open so from where my mother-in-law was sitting she could see my daughter nursing."

"She was talking to me about how I would just have to get used to nursing in front of people because no one looks."

Just then my daughter started moving around and lost the nipple, but I got her back to it and my mother-in-law said, "Oh, she's got it again."

"That entire time my mother-in-law was telling me no one would be looking at me, she was looking at my boobs the whole time! Yuck!"

Serina, Age 23

"For my mother-in-law's birthday the entire Anderson family went to Las Vegas. It just happened to be my mother-in-law's birthday; everyone was just planning a vacation that weekend. My daughter was about three months old and I knew the whole time I would be in my hotel room taking care of her, while my mother-in-law continued to try and steal my husband Richard from me. She has always tried to interfere in my relationship with my husband."

We got to Vegas and immediately she was ordering us around, "I want to go here, I want to go there." Then she said, "Richard you and I can go out tonight while Nina stays with the baby."

"I didn't mind watching our baby but I didn't want my husband hanging out with his mom all night. Plus there were plenty of other people for her to hang out with, cousins, and aunts. Oh, and let's not forget that she can hang out with her own darn husband! The birthday girl gets what the birthday girl wants. So that night my husband, my mother-in-law, his cousin, and his aunts and uncles all went to see a show and have dinner. I walked around by myself, but luckily Richard's cousin came by my hotel and we watched a movie that night. Richard came back to the room at about three in the morning. I guess he and his mom were gambling."

I just kept thinking to myself, "Only two more nights".

"The next day we all had brunch together and went to the pool. Then we saw all the different hotels and did some shopping. It was getting late and my mother-in-law heard about another show that she wanted to see. So all the relatives got ready to go. No one offered to watch my daughter and let me have a little vacation, not that they had to but it would have been nice. My husband told me that he wasn't going to the show but wanted to gamble with his brother and cousins and promised me I could go out the next night. Richard showed up to the hotel room very late and like any worried wife in Vegas I waited up for him. The next day all the family did some more activities together and gambled."

"That night was our last night and it was my turn to go out. My husband's cousin Michelle wanted to go to this hotel and take pictures. It's her tradition to take pictures at this hotel every time she is in Vegas. So I said I would go with her. The only problem was that it was on the other end of the strip. We were going to walk it anyway. I fed the baby so she didn't need to eat for another three hours. I gave Richard ideas on what to do if she started crying, like walk up and down the halls to put her to sleep or give her a bath. So away Michelle and I went to the other end of the strip. It took us about a half an hour to get there. We took some pictures, got a few slices of pizza then made our way back. We were so tired from walking. We saw one of those bike-cart deals, the ones where the people cart you around like a taxi, and we decided to take it. It was the most fun I had the entire time! They couldn't bike us all the way home so we still had a long walk. We finally got back to the hotel about an hour and a half later. I was walking down the hall to my room and saw my mother-in-law coming out of my room and going into hers. I felt sick. I knew by the terrible look on her face that she was mad. (Most likely at me.) I got to my room and the baby was crying on the bed with Richard. I picked the baby up and nursed her back to sleep."

I asked Richard what his mom was doing in the room. He got mad at me and said, "She was here because the baby wouldn't stop crying!"

I said, "Honey did you do anything I told you to do to put her to bed?"

He replied a bit sheepishly, "No, no I didn't."

I said, "I guess you have no reason to be mad at me then."

Then he said, "I was mad because my mom said she thought the baby was hungry."

I asked him, "Didn't you see me feed her for a half an hour right before I left?"

"I suppose it isn't Richard's fault, like I said his mother would do and say anything to create conflict between us. The next morning we were packing to go home and I was walking the baby around to keep her happy. My husband's aunt and uncle had their door slightly opened. They are Michelle's parents. I was walking passed there room and heard my mother-in-law sounding angry about something. I continued listening and figured out right away that she was mad at me."

I heard her say, "Nina is an awful mother leaving her baby like that! Then she said, "She was gone for hours and just left her screaming daughter with Richard!"

When she said that I opened the door fully and walked in and looked right at her saying, "No, the thing is that Richard did none of the things I told him to do to make the baby happy, he just sat with her."

"By now my heart was pumping out of my chest."

My mother-in-law snapped back at me, "So what, you still shouldn't have been gone so long!"

I was mad now and said, "I was gone for an hour and a half, and that is the longest time I have been away from her this entire trip!" plus I fed her right before we left!"

Richard's mom just kept laying into me, "Well, you still should have left Richard a bottle, what kind of mother are you!"

Thank goodness at that point Richard's aunt stepped in and took my side, "Richard is going to have to learn how to handle his own baby." Then she told my mother-in-law, "I do remember Michelle coming home only an hour and a half later."

"I shook my head and then left. I had to get away from my mother-in-law. I was pretty mad that the one night, or should I say the one hour and a half I had to myself I am suddenly a terrible parent. She is the dysfunctional parent if she has raised four kids and doesn't know a way to make a baby happy. I will never go on a vacation with her again!"

Nina, Age 25

"My husbands mother is a mean person. She is always badmouthing me to other people. Even in front of me! She will say things to my husband like he should never have married me.

The biggest thing she likes to say to my husband about me is, "You know her genes are wipe out genes, and none of your kids will look like us because of it!" Then she always ends it with, "They all will just look like, short, fat McClouds."

"I can't believe she has the guts to say stuff like that. She has always been a dominant woman and I am much more submissive. It has gotten pretty bad over the years and so I just never talk to her. I never go over there anymore."

Sasha, Age 30

"My husband gained 45 lbs. when I got pregnant. We ate all the time because I was always hungry. My mother-in-law always tells him, in front of me, and anyone else that is around, that it's my fault he gained weight."

She says to my husband, "You know why you gained this weight don't you?"

She told him it was because all he ate was junk food. Then she always throws in a jab at the end like, "Not to mention the fact that your wife can't cook."

"I cook great food, but we also go out to healthy restaurants. It was only because we ate a lot of food all the time that he gained the weight. She can't speak for her self because they always get fast food and she only knows how to make one dish. I know it's a superiority issue and she wants to seem better at everything than me. I can't stand the women!"

Gail, Age 24

"I believe in the hidden meaning behind what my mother-in-law says. For instance whenever I bring my 6month-old daughter over to her house she will be in the other room talking to the baby saying, 'Tell *momma* what? Tell *momma* what?"

"I thought she was saying *momma* on accident but it happed all the time and my daughter started calling my mother-in-law *momma*!"

My husband would correct my daughter and tell her, "Say hi *grandma*."

Even after my husband told his mom to stop saying momma, in front of our daughter, she would still say, "Awww show momma," or, "Give momma a hug."

"After weeks of this I was beginning to wonder, but I still gave her the benefit of the doubt. Then when we went over there again she took my daughter from me and my daughter started to cry."

My mother-in-law said to my little girl, "Oh do you want Trisha?" She handed my daughter to me and said, "Here, go to Trisha."

"She was telling my daughter in a very subtle way to call me by my first name!"

Normal people would say, "Go to mommy."

"My mother-in-law started pulling that same stunt often. I would try to correct her by saying, 'Yeah, come to mommy.' I think my mother-in-law is a little crazy and I think it is weird that she is trying to teach my daughter to call her momma. I don't ever leave my daughter alone with my mother-in-law anymore."

Trisha, Age 32

"Years ago, when I was still a young mother, I was visiting my in-laws with my four month old son. I always kept him in little mittens when I didn't cut his fingers so he would not scratch himself. I also would hold him a lot whenever I was at my in-laws because he wasn't used to a lot of people around him and he would get scared and cry. When I was at my in-laws house I saw my mother-in-law outside talking to a neighbor who had a baby around the same age as mine so I went outside to talk to them."

I walked up to them and my mother-in-law said to the neighbor, "This is my daughter-in-law Sharon and her son." Then she said to the neighbor, "She is the one I was telling you about. See how her son wears those ridicules mittens!" They chuckled and then my mother-in-law said, "He will never be able to hold anything in those." She went on to say to the neighbor, (with me still standing right there!) "She also never puts him on the ground, and I am sure the poor boy will never learn how to crawl."

"I was standing there feeling completely mortified. I felt like I was a horrible mother or something. I tried harder to teach him how to crawl and I kept the mittens off of him. The next time I was at my mother-in-law's house my son scratched his face so severely that he still has a scar. I should have never cared about what she said. He is my son and I know what's best for him."

Christie, Age 49

"My daughter is fifteen months old and tries to copy anything we say. She is actually very good. She can say some things very clearly. My mother-in-law is jealous of the fact that my daughter is smarter than her other grand children. One of her other granddaughters are seven months older then my daughter and she can't say anything."

"She got so jealous one time when I told my daughter to say sorry for something she had done wrong."

My daughter quickly said, "Sobby."

"She at least was trying to say it right. Sobby is good enough for me, but my mother-in-law was so jealous that she could say anything at all that she started to make fun of how my little girl had said the word sorry."

My mother-in-law kept saying over and over in a sarcastic tone, "Anna, are you sobby? Huh, Ana? Are you sobby?" Then she said, "I think that's just so funny how she says sobby instead of sorry."

"My mother-in-law just started making fun of my daughter's attempts at speaking all the time after that. I finally said something about it after a month or so."

I pulled her aside and said, "Okay, I have heard you say it is funny like a million times!"

"Then I told her that I thought it was great that Anna could even say as much as she does, and I asked my mother-in-law if she would please stop laughing at Anna. She stopped but did pout for quite a long time after that."

Sandy, Age 35

"I have three kids, twin daughters who are seven and a son who is four. My husband and I both come from big families so our children have a lot of cousins to play with. One Easter after all the kids were done finding their Easter eggs in grandma and grandpa's back yard, a few of the kids wanted to play hide and seek. My in-laws have a huge house so the kids always had a great time finding great hiding places. My daughters gave me my son to hold so he wouldn't follow them when they hid. I was in the living room talking with my husband and a few of his aunts and uncles. My daughters went up into my mother and father-in-law's room and hid under their bed. They waited a while but no one was finding them. They were getting ready to leave when my mother-in-law Sue walked in with Max. Max is Sue's sister's husband and my husband's Uncle Max."

They were talking about the party and then Sue said, "I can't stand Christina. (Me) I don't have a clue why my son married her. She is such a bimbo."

Uncle Max said, "Don't be jealous."

Sue said, "You would like her! Then she laughed and said, "In fact, you probably like her even more than me!"

"Then, with my poor daughters looking from under the dust ruffle, my mother-in-law proceeded to kiss Uncle Max!"

My daughters came out from under the bed. (Thank goodness they came out before anything else happened) and said, "Um, grandma?"

My daughters had completely surprised my mother-in-law and she sputtered, "Uh girls, um what are you doing in here?" She was scared out of her wits!

My oldest twin daughter replied, "We were playing a game of hide and go seek. Sorry grandma."

"We'd better go down stairs and find your mom and dad." My mother-in-law said.

"My husband and I were still talking to everyone when they all came down stairs. My mother-in-law asked if we would see her in the garage. Then she found her husband and asked him to go into the garage also. There we all were my husband and I, my twin girls, my father and mother-in-law and Uncle Max. My mother-in-law looked horrified. I could see she was gathering her thoughts."

My father-in-law asked, "What is all this? What's going on?"

Then Sue slowly began to say, "Well, the girls were playing a game and over-heard some things I said about Christina."

We just stood there waiting, not sure what this was all about, and then Sue continued, "They also saw some things, and um, well, the truth is that I have been having an affair with Max for three years."

"Then my husband and my father-in-law started yelling at Sue and Max. Soon everyone was yelling. I took my daughters out to the rest of the party."

When we were in the house someone asked my daughters what happened. They said, "Grandma was kissing Uncle Max".

"Soon everyone was talking. I felt bad but I didn't care too much that my daughters said anything because my mother-in-law has gossiped so much about me. Everyone would have found out sooner or later. My husband and I had taken two cars to the party so I just left all the chaos and took my kids home. My father and mother-in-law got divorced. My husband was so mad at his mom that we haven't seen her for six months."

Christina, Age 46

"My mother-in-law has never like me. When I had my son she would never come and visit. We only live fifteen minutes away. At first I thought she just didn't like babies but a year later her daughter had a baby boy and my mother-in-law has never left the baby's side. Every time we would get together for holidays she would say how my sister-in-laws baby was the best baby on earth. For Christmas she would buy my sister-in-law's son so many nice things. She never gave my son anything that wasn't already used. She would sometimes put an old ratty toy in a big name brand box. Its very sad that just because she doesn't like me that she hates my child too."

Mara, Age 27

"With our new baby my mother-in-law knows I go to bed by 10pm. She also knows that sometimes my husband stays up later than I do. For the past few weeks she has been calling at eleven thirty or twelve at night just so she can talk to my husband. She will make up things sometimes just to get him interested in the conversation and they will talk for a long time."

If she ever calls late and he doesn't answer she will leave a message saying, "Hi Luke, and family. One time she left a message and said, "Hi Luke and Jamie this is grandma, Luke I just wanted to tell you that grandpa's birthday is this weekend and I was wondering if you might want to go out with us. We will be going to a very nice restaurant. Don't worry I will pay for you. Bye Luke, I love you."

"First of all if this woman had any etiquette at all she would continue to address us both and not single Luke out at the end to say she loves! Second, why doesn't she treat my husband and I equally?"

For example, why didn't she say, "Luke and Jamie, would you like to go to grandpa's birthday party?" Why didn't she say, "Bye guy's love you both?"

Jamie, Age 31

"I have been with my husband for five years. In all that time she has been a complete roller coaster. At first she started out calm and nice, she then did some not so great things but it would go up and down. Some weeks she would be sweet some weeks she would be the devil. I thought after being with her son this long she would have laid off a little. I actually feel after all these years its worse than ever. My husband said she probably hates me because I never ask for help with the babies. I realized that was a big part of it. She treats her daughter very well because she is always asking for help. That is her biological daughter though. Whenever I do ask her for help she never helps me. I wish I could just forget about the little things that she does to get at me. I was talking to my friend the other day and she told me to yell at her when she does that stuff. I told her that it is too hard because my mother-in-law is so sneaky about it that I can't confront her about things without me sounding like the bad guy."

Roxanne, Age 32

"My sister-in-law is getting married this spring and I will be one of her brides-maids. We all had to go try on bridesmaid's dresses and it took all day. I had my son with me the entire time we were running around in the stores, and my husband was home with his mom. Neither my husband nor my mother-in-law had offered to watch my son. My son is two and can run fast. Although, we didn't know it would have taken all day so I don't blame my husband too much. While some of the other girls were trying on dresses I went next door to a bagel shop to get a snack for my son so he would be a little happier. He only took a few bites then ran around some more. So I kept the bagel in my purse for him for later. We finally got to leave after hours, and hours. I drove to my mother-in-law's house because that's where my husband was. When we got there my son kept asking for food so I went into my purse to get the rest of the bagel."

My husband quickly said, "Don't give him that here, my mom just had a long talk with me about how you let Austin eat everywhere in the house and he spills his crumbs all over."

"I was so mad because I never give him snacks in her house. We almost never even go to her house. I let it go because I was starting to get mad. I took my son outside and gave him some bagel. When we came back in my son wanted to sit with my father-in-law and have my father-in-law read him a book. My mother-in-law must have been jealous because she went into her cupboard and pulled out a handful of cookie wafers. (Which are extremely crumbly.) I couldn't believe she would complain about me to my husband and then give my son something ten times messier! I think she wanted to blame me for her crumbs! She keeps her house pretty clean so she needed someone to blame for the tiny things she missed. What a weirdo!"

Molly, Age 23

"I can't believe how different people can be. I was raised with a mother who loves kids and anytime I needed her to baby-sit she would. I don't get along with my mother-in-law but I still bring my daughter over to see her a lot. She always tells me that I never ask her to baby-sit. I trust my mom with my daughter more then I trust my mother-in-law, but I still don't even have my mom watch my daughter much. One time we were at my in-laws and my brother-in-law asked us if we wanted to go to a movie. I said that we could if his mom wanted to watch my daughter."

My sister-in-law over heard this and got angry and said, "No, mom is going to watch James tonight."

"My sister-in-law has an awful little son. James is three and my daughter is fifteen months. James is so mean to my daughter. If she is playing with something he will take it and hide it from her. If they go into the other room he will hurt her. My sister-in-law never punishes James for hurting my daughter."

"Another time I wanted my mother-in-law to watch my daughter she said she would watch her only if my daughter was a sleep."

I said, "Okay I will put her down for a nap and you can watch her, because I have to go to the store."

She started to get nervous and said, "I would but she is being annoying today."

"My daughter was fine and she was about to go to sleep! I don't know why my mother-in-law even asks to baby-sit. Then I realized that my mother-in-law always tells people I never let her watch my daughter, but she actually doesn't want to, she just wants to tell everyone that I never let her. Psycho!"

LeeAnne, Age 26

"My mother-in-law always disagrees with how I am raising my sons. I have one son who is five and one who is only eight months. I let my eight-month-old son sleep with me still and I had my five-year-old sleep with me until he was two years old. I just think that it is the most natural thing to let your baby sleep with you. I have friends who disagree with me also. I don't have to work so I understand why when mothers do work that it is best for the child to sleep in their own room. I would most likely do what they are doing too. The way I do it is hard sometimes. Any way one day I had a friend who got in a car accident and was in the emergency room. My husband was at work and I didn't want to bring my baby to the ER, so I asked my mother-in-law if she could watch him. She said she would so I rushed to her house with my son. I told her the best way to put him to sleep was to ride him in the car or walk him in the stroller. I told her he would fall asleep instantly if she did any one of those things. I got to the hospital and my friend's parents who had called me earlier told me she was now in a coma. They were so upset; they thought she wasn't going to make it. I was in shock. I stayed with them for three hours. I kept calling my mother-in-law from my cell phone asking how my son was. She said he was fine and had fallen asleep. I waited a little longer with them then went to my in-laws. I heard my son balling and I ran upstairs. He was in the bathroom in his playpen in the pitch dark. When I picked him up he was shaking like crazy. I called out for my mother-in-law and she didn't answer. I walked around the house then saw her in the back yard gardening. I was so mad!"

I yelled to her "I'm back, why was Aiden in the bathroom?"

She said, "I know you have your methods, and I have mine." "You know I never wanted to put him to bed that way."

If I knew you were going to do that I wouldn't have let you watch him." I said.

"I was furious! I grabbed his things and walked out the front door."

As I was putting my son in his car seat my mother-in-law's neighbor came up to me and said, "I was getting worried because I heard your baby crying for three hours straight."

"I thanked her for telling me then left. I didn't go back to my in-laws for months and never ever let her watch my son again."

Courtney, Age 33

"I am pretty cautious when it comes to letting my three week old daughter be around people who are sick. She was premature and the doctor said she could catch something easier then most babies. So I always tell my family and my husbands family if anyone is sick please don't get to close to the baby. My family understands but my in-laws don't. They say it helps build the immune system. That's all fine and good but I don't think exposing a newborn to flu is the smartest thing. I think I am getting ahead of myself. It all happened on Christmas Eve. We were planning on going to my in-laws that night and my family's house Christmas day. My husband and I knew the flu was going around town so we stayed home a lot. We called my husbands parents to make sure that everyone was well."

My mother-in-law got on the phone and said, "Yeah, everyone is fine come over as soon as you can."

"So we got all our things ready and went to there house early. When we got there we were greeted with our usual hugs from everyone. Everyone was kissing the baby."

We were there about four hours before my sister-in-law said, "I'm going to take a nap I still don't feel good. You want to take one too Eric?" Talking to her husband.

I looked at them and my husband and said, "You're sick?"

She said, "Yeah, it's the fever flu."

I was so angry! "We all hugged you! You kissed my newborn! We asked mom if any one wasn't feeling good and she said everyone was fine!"

My brother-in-law Eric who is a doctor said, "Oh she won't get it."

Then my mother-in-law said, "The reason I didn't say anything was because I wanted to see my son and granddaughter on Christmas Eve and I knew you wouldn't come if I told you people were sick."

For the first time I broke down crying and sobbed, "What you all did was wrong, and you have probably given my daughter the flu." I couldn't stop crying.

"You know she has a weak immune system and could get very sick!" Everyone was quiet no one said anything. I just stood there staring at them and then I finally said, "I hope you're all happy!"

"I immediately went home. When I got home I tried to wash her off and I took a shower. Three days later it hit us. I had the worst fever I had ever had in my life, and my poor daughter was so sick that I had to take her to the hospital. The doctors weren't sure if she was going to live. So there I was, with what I thought was a dying child, just because my mother-in-law wanted to be selfish. I told myself I would never talk to that woman again if my daughter died. I had never felt so much pain and hate in my whole life. I waited and waited and finally the doctors said her fever went down and she was going to live. I was so happy. I hadn't stopped crying that whole time, my daughter got better though. I cherished her even more then ever. I have forgiven my mother in-law but I still haven't forgotten. I have not had the strength to go to her house and I don't think I could ever look at her in the same way again."

Ashley, Age 25

Let's Review

- The most important thing to know when dealing with your kids and your mother-in-law is to do whatever you know is best for your children. You will know what is best and never ever let any one pressure or make you feel bad about your decisions.

- Know this is yet another reason your mother-in-law will be getting jealous. She knows you and "her son" are officially growing your *own* family.

Gross, Sick, & Just Pathetic

◆

Part 8: Okay Now It's Ridiculous!

To me this stuff is plain disgusting. By now you have read some of the outrageous things that mothers-in-law do. These new stories are gross and a desperate attempt of a mother-in-law trying to take back her son.

"My mother-in-law almost acts, no she does act, like we are two girls in school fighting over the same guy. Her favorite thing to do is tell my husband that she watches all the shows he watches. My husband also loves this radio program that talks about conspiracies and UFOs. One day he was talking to my brother-in-law about the show and like always she butts in and says, "Oh that's my favorite program!""

"Now the thing is she is a strong Catholic and when my husband and I were just dating I would hear her talk about that stuff as bogus and sacrilegious. (But the woman does have to win back her boyfriend!)"

Anyway, my husband Mark was mad, and said, "What are you talking about you have never talked about liking UFOs or anything."

Then she starts to smile and flirt (with her own son, yuck!) And said, "You think you have everyone in this family figured out, but you don't know me at all."

"She was acting mysterious and hard to get. Double *yuck*!"

April, Age 26

"One New Years Eve my husband and I were going to have a party at our house. We had left some of our champagne glasses at my in-laws house on Christmas. I had a few of my friends over helping get the party ready. My friends wanted to take a break and go to my in-laws with my husband and I to get the glasses. It took us about thirty minutes to get there. We got to my in-laws and didn't see anyone. I was hoping my mother-in-law wasn't there. But unfortunately she was. She prances down the stairs and gives my husband a kiss. We explained why we were there."

She was looking at my husband and said, "Are those the pants you got for Christmas? They look a little tight in the crotch. Let me check something."

Then, in front of all my friends and me she preceded to put her hand down his pants and feel around. "Well, it feels like you might have enough room."

"I wanted to puke! I looked at all my friends who were smirking."

My husband just said, "My pants are fine."

"I want him to tell her that's just not right. He is thirty years old for goodness sake! My friends have never let him live it down."

Mindy, Age 30

"My family is very conservative. They are very proper and never talk about sex. My husband's family is more open with talking about everything. Which can be good and bad. One day, my little brother, my mom, my mother-in-law, and I all went shopping together. We stopped for some lunch at this French restaurant. We were having a good conversation when my mother-in-law started talking about my husband's and my sex life. She said that she had something for me. She pulled out this sexual stimulant lubricant from her purse. My mom sat there with her eyes wide in shock. My brother who is twelve had the biggest smirk on his face. My mother-in-law kept on talking about how great it works. I was drinking my wine pretty fast. I just nodded my head. I knew my mom was repulsed. My mom was looking around the room to see if people were listening. I don't blame my mom because my mother-in-law was talking pretty loud."

My mother-in-law then said, "The next time you have sex with Peter you call me right after and tell me how it went."

"I drank faster and faster. I wanted to pass out! My poor brother and mom! I know I will never have them hang out again!"

Rowena, Age 22

"My mother-in-law walks around naked in front of my husband. My husband and I were at my in-laws and he said for me to wait downstairs while he was going to get something upstairs. He ran upstairs and my mother-in-law started talking to him while she was in the shower. Then she got out of the shower and was walking around naked. My husband says she does that all the time. I think it doesn't faze him because he is used to it. I don't know if it's just me, or if it is the way I was raised, but that doesn't seem right. I am pretty grossed out by it actually."

Deana, Age 30

"When ever we go to family functions and see my husbands mother she will not leave my husband's side. My mother-in-law will follow him around the entire time. She will hug him or put her arm through his. If they are sitting on the couch she will have her hands on his leg. I won't even get into how she squeezes her way in-between my husband and I if we are close to each other. The sickest thing she does though is when we are saying goodbye she will grab my husbands face and kiss him for a while on the lips. It creeps me out. She doesn't do it to her daughters and she always kisses him right next to me. I might understand if it was a short kiss on the lips but hers are long and disgusting."

Mimi, Age 34

"My husband and I have huge families. I come from a family of seven kids, and he comes from a family of six. His parents also have many brothers and sisters. When we get together for the holidays the house is packed. On Christmas we usually wait until the extended families have all gone home to open the presents with just my husband's family. I have been married to my husband for four years now and things with his mother have not been so good. She doesn't like me at all but she acts like the sweetest person to me around other people so know one understands why I say she doesn't like me. She goes to church at least three times a week and sings in the church choir. So in everyone's eyes she is a saint. From what I have seen she is a gossipy mean woman. Anyway, this Christmas she decided that everyone should open their presents while all the extended families were still there. So everyone gathered into the living room to watch us open our gifts. I got some candles and soaps.

Which is great but then my mother-in-law came up to me and shouted to everyone, "Okay, everyone Veronica is opening her presents."

"All the cousins, aunts, uncles, grandparents are all watching me. I didn't know why she didn't put attention on me when I opened my other gifts. I was opening the bag and pulled out some lacy thongs. No one said anything."

I was thinking to myself, "Great everyone is so embarrassed for me." Then I said out loud, "Wow, thanks mom."

My mother-in-law then said, "Oh, wait there's one more." She pulls out another present.

"I start to open it and I was happy because it felt like a board game and I knew it would divert the attention off the lacy thongs. Which is sick of a mother-in-law to give if you don't have that kind of relationship. She just wanted to embarrass me. It did work though. So I am opening the board game and found it was not a normal board game it was some kind of sex game, with whips and all. I was mortified."

I acted like it was funny and said, "*All right!* Look honey now we can have some fun tonight!"

"I felt like I was going to pass out! She is disgusting! I think she just wants to be a part of her son's sex life any way she can."

Veronica, Age 25

"My husband and I have a small apartment and an even smaller closet. My mother-in-law tries to buy my husband's love with clothes and other gifts. She did this the most right after we were married. My husband's grandmother likes to buy us clothes and stuff as well at garage sales for cheap. My mother-in-law knows I am in the family but doesn't treat me like I am. She always buys stuff for my husband. If my grandmother-in-law buys something for me and asks my mother-in-law to give it to me she won't. She will give it to one of her daughters or throw it away. I told my mother-in-law and my grandmother-in-law not to buy us any more clothes because we don't have the room in our small apartment. My grandmother-in-law listens to me but not my mother-in-law."

The worst is when my husband wears the things my mother-in-law gives him in front of her because she will then say, "That's the shirt I got you isn't it?" And "I have the best taste, that looks so good on you."

"She does that all the time. It's almost like she is gloating because he is wearing the things she got him and nothing I got him or he got himself. After I told her to stop buying my husband things, she started buying him even more. One day my husband's favorite shirt that he got from his grandfather ripped to the point were it could not be fixed. I felt bad for him and his birthday was coming the next week. So I went out and found him a shirt that was almost identical. He was so happy I found him the shirt that he took off the shirt he was wearing and put the one I got him on. Since it was his birthday his mom wanted us to go out with her and my father-in-law. We met them at the restaurant and they had already been seated. We walked up to them at their table. We gave our hello hugs."

She then noticed his shirt. She started to get mad and forcefully said, "Where did you get that shirt?" "Who gave it to you?" Her voice started to get louder.

My husband said, "Brittany got it for me because my old one of grandpa's ripped."

In the middle of the restaurant she started yelling, "So you don't like all the shirt's I bought you!" Then she screamed, "You love that bitch but you don't even love your own *Mother!*"

At that point I stood up and yelled, "Listen you rude old women, don't ever call me a bitch again!" I grabbed my purse and fired back at her, "The only bitch I see in this room is you, and you can just go back to your sad and negative life, and believe me I will never be a part of it again."

"Then I walked out the door. My husband followed me. I haven't seen her in a year. I feel good about it. I am not going to ever let her negativity get me down! That scene at the restaurant was completely out of line."

Brittany, Age 30

"I never knew why my mother-in-law liked me more then her other daugh-ters-in-law. Don't get me wrong she still doesn't like me but she treats me slightly better then her other daughters-in-law. I finally figured it out when one of her girlfriends told me that my mother-in-law tells everyone she meets that I look just like her and that the only reason her son married me was because he loves his mom and wanted to find someone just like her. I started to feel sick. I did remember her saying something of that nature before. From that point forward I always would listen to her at holidays when she would talk to people. She did in fact talk about me as her twin. She would say it all the time."

She said things like, "Frank has a great relationship with Summer because he has such an amazing relationship with me," and "She doesn't have the best personality but Frank was more going for the look and body of a woman. That's why he picked Summer, she has my body and look." Summer and I were blessed with similar boobs too. I'm sure Frank likes that!"

"I am sure people do look for similar features in their spouse as in their family but she doesn't have to keep talking about it being her boobs that Frank likes!"

Summer, Age 24

"After all the weird and psychotic things my mother-in-law has done to me I shouldn't think she would ever stop. We go to visit her on occasion, but like I said she has done some sick things in the past and that's why we go on *slight* occasion. Anyhow, my parents-in-law have a spa and my husband and I like to go in it once in a while when we go over to their house. When we left my husband forgot to get his sweatshirt from their house. He loves his sweatshirt and so he called his mom to tell her that he left his sweatshirt at the house. She already knew he had and told him she would take it and put it by the door for him. He went over the next day to get it. He thanked his mom for keeping it safe and then went on his way. He came home and I could smell his mom. I thought it was just from him being in their house, but I smelled him and the smell wasn't coming from him. I opened the bag his sweatshirt was in and the smell was overwhelming. I am guessing that his mom actually sprayed her perfume onto his sweatshirt so he would think about her. I even felt wet spots where the perfume was sprayed. It took so long to get the smell off that thing. At this point I just don't know what to say about her."

Casey, Age 33

"My husband likes to work out but he is not that tone. Whenever we see my mother-in-law she always moves me to the side and grabs my husband's butt."

She will say things like, "Yeah that's a nice ass," Or "Your butt is so firm!" while she is grabbing his butt.

"She will even come behind him while he is talking to people and slap his butt. I am so grossed out by it. I told my husband that it makes me uncomfortable. I said that he shouldn't let her do it anymore, especially in front of me."

So now every time she does it he will say things like, "Okay, mom that's enough."

"She usually gets it and won't do it as often. I wouldn't care as much if she didn't do it right in front of me!"

Candace, Age 25

"I love to visit with my in-laws. Everyone, that is, except my mother-in-law. It's not that she is a bad person per say, but she is a little crazy when it comes to her boys. She does weird things to get my husbands attention. For example they have a bit of money and have there own tennis and basketball courts. My husband loves to play basketball on the weekends with his brother and father. I go to cheer him on. His mom also is there to cheer him on. When my husband, father, and brother-in-law were done with their game my mother-in-law started to freak out. She had lost her keys somewhere around the court. We all had to look for them. We looked on the grass, on the court, everywhere. She then asked my husband to look for them with her in the bushes. (Which were about five feet from anything). They were looking and talking for about twenty minutes. Then I saw her pull them out of her pocket and toss them into the bushes. All that looking we did was for nothing. She told my husband to look in the area that she had just tossed them. Sure enough he found them! She told him she would have to take him to dinner for saving her life. (Its not like she didn't have a spare car key). In the house I told my husband what I saw. He got mad that he had to spend all that time looking for nothing."

So he went up to her and firmly asked his mother, "Did you have your keys all along?"

She quickly replied, "Is that what your whore told you?" Then she yelled, "It's a lie! She just wants to break us up!"

"My husband did remember looking in that spot before and was a little perplexed when he found the keys the second time. He told him mom to calm down and never to call me a whore again. At least he stands up for me, which is more than some husbands do for their wives."

Naomi, Age 21

Final Review On Mother-in-law's

- If things get bad don't think you have to stick around for more punishment. You have the choice to be with her as little or as much as YOU want.

- Go to a counselor. It could be a church counselor or a professional therapist. There is no reason for you to try and fix everything on your own. If things get bad enough for you to want to go to someone who can help you then go. Don't sit around and think about doing it and never go because you will only continue to hurt.

- Remember you can never change someone like your mother-in-law; you can only change the way you react to them. The best way to react is positively and you will most always have the upper hand.

- Calmly tell yourself, "She too was once a baby". It might make you feel a little more like she is only a human and not a demon.

- Everything she is doing is just an attempt to get your husband's attention. You may not have seen it as much before because she didn't realize how many things have changed. He has grown up and isn't a kid anymore.

- Some of the more perverse stories could be her way to show that he is still "her" little boy and she may not realize what she is doing or maybe she is sick and messed up.

How To Be A Good
Mother-in-law

✦

Part 9: Make The Difference

After all that we are now going to talk about how we are not going to make the mistakes our mothers-in-law made. We can change the legacy of the bad mother-in-law. Remember how bad you felt when your mother-in-law treated you like dirt; well you are not going to let that happen with your daughter-in-law or son-in-law. We will fight back and try our best to be all that we can be as good mothers-in-law and break the cycle!

How to be a good mother-in-law

- The number one thing I would say to be a good mother-in-law is to give the couple space. Meaning, don't pry or ask too many questions about their life. Let them come to you.

- The second thing I would say is to treat your new daughter-in-law as if she were your own child. If you do something for one you better do it for the other.

- Thirdly I would say give the new couple some slack, they are starting there own family and they might not always do everything the way you always did.

- Never put down your new daughter or son-in-law. You never know how sensitive they are. You have to remember that you both come from different upbringings.

- Put your foot down if necessary. Just because they need space doesn't mean they can disrespect you, especially in your own home.

- Be honest. Tell the truth if they ask but be gentle with feelings.

- Be supportive and friendly.

- Don't hang all over your son, especially in front of her. (This means no more butt grabbing!)

The Bad Daughters

◆

Part 10: Don't Think It's Just Mother-in-law's!

If you are a mother with a bad mother-in-law and a bad daughter-in-law, don't worry it's not just you. I have many friends who have awful mother-in-law's and bad daughter-in-law's. I would have written about how bad daughters-in-law can cause trouble but the majority of stories I collected were about bad mother-in-law's. I myself have not experienced a bad daughter-in-law, but I never said they aren't out there. Here are a few stories about some bad daughter-in-law's.

"My daughter-in-law wanted to get a boob job. I told her she could do what ever she wanted it's her body. I told her she looked fine the way she was so if she didn't want to she didn't have to. She just smiled and left. My daughter-in-law went home to her husband, my son, crying hysterically. She told him that I said I thought she would look like a slut if she got a boob job. She also told him I said she would look even fatter than she was if she did it. She cried and cried. He called me up and yelled at me. He called me all kinds of names. I tried to explain myself but he didn't believe me. He never talked to me much after that. About one year later he found out that his wife had been cheating on him throughout their entire marriage. He found out that she also lied about a lot of other things as well and he felt so bad that he didn't believe me. They got divorced and now he is dating a nice girl."

Cynthia, Age 60

"I was at home when my son and daughter-in-law came to visit me. They had brought over lunch and rented a movie for us to watch. We ate lunch and then were watching the movie when my daughter-in-law had to go to the rest room. I saw her out of the corner of my eye pick up my purse and bring it to the bath-room with her. I didn't know what to say. I just sat there and watched the movie, waiting for her to come out. Sure enough she came slowly out of the rest room with my purse. She put it back where she found it, but I was curious if she took anything out. I didn't want to go over and look through it right then and there so I waited. I got the opportunity when they went for a walk. I looked around and everything seemed to be there. I opened my wallet and all my money was gone. I always kept at least twenty dollars in my wallet at all times. She had stolen from me. I never said anything, but I also hid my purse from then on. I hope I can fig-ure something out with her."

Mary Jo, Age 57

"My son married young but so did I so I can't say anything. My son and daughter-in-law both attend the same college I went to. My daughter is majoring in the same subject that I did so I told her if she ever needed help that I would gladly help her. One day she called up and asked if I could help her with a paper she had to write. She just wanted me to re-read it and tell her what she should maybe do differently. I told her that it would be fine and to come over as soon as she wanted. So we set it up and she came over. I read her paper and thought it was excellent. I told her a few things she might want to do to make it better. She said that they were great ideas. Then she started to cry and sat on my couch in a ball."

I said, "What's wrong honey?"

She screamed, "I hate that you will never be my mom, *never!*"

"I know she didn't have the best relationship with her own mother but I can't for the life of me figure out why she had that episode. I am still so confused."

Aleece, Age 50

"I was gone on a business trip and came home and saw that my son and daughter-in-law had a party in my house. They have a small apartment so I guess they needed a bigger house to have a party in. I saw some broken beer glasses in the yard and I actually found a bong in my bedroom. I was so mad. I called them up and yelled at them. My daughter-in-law hates me now and my son barely comes over."

Kathy, Age 48

"My daughter-in-law seemed so nice. I thought we had a good relationship. My daughter-in-law was always polite and we liked to have a mother-daughter day once in a while. I myself had a bad mother-in-law so I wanted to do everything I could to have a good relationship with her. Just when I thought everything was going so well, my niece told me that my daughter-in-law was spreading rumors about me. She would tell lies about what happened when we were together. She also told my mother-in-law things that made my mother-in-law very happy to know. I was getting hit at every angle. I just give up!"

Jolene, Age 52

Okay, that's about all I could dig up on bad daughters-in-law but I am sure there are plenty more stories out there. We can just save it for my next book. To help anyone with similar problems such as the lying or spreading rumors I would advise you to stay honest and don't let the lies get to you too much. As we can see in Cynthia's case the truth finally came out. Most of the time it does. Your true friends know when someone is making something up about you.

In Aleece's story she may have thought she was being helpful and the daughter-in-law mistook something she said. You have to explain if you said something that was taken out of context. You could say I think I said that wrong thing or you might have misunderstood me.

In Kathy's case her son and daughter-in-law were being disrespectful and trashing her house. Kathy did everything right by yelling at them. So what if they hate you for a bit. Put your foot down if necessary. Just because they need space doesn't mean they can disrespect you. Especially in your own home!

How To Deal With Him

✦

Part 11: Ways To Help Your Marriage

There has already been a lot of advice on dealing with your husband, such as, don't talk his ears off about his mother and all the things she has done to you. He cares about you but he doesn't understand how women are because he is a man. Don't expect he will side with you when you are talking about his family in a negative way, even if you feel you have the right to. He could get defensive and angry and turn it around to what is wrong with you and your family!

Don't expect your husband to stop caring about his mom even if you don't care much for her. He will always love her because she is his mom and she raised him. She cares about him too even though she dislikes you. Keep in mind though; that there may be times when a family is so dysfunctional that if the husband is still fine with the way things are there may be a problem with him as well. Your husband should be strong enough not to support disruptive behavior just because it is in his family.

My main point for having a "How To Deal With Him" section was not to talk about him, his mom, and you, but more importantly about *him* and *you*. The two of you are a couple not him and his mom. The man must leave his family and become a new family with his wife.

So your next goal is to make your marriage perfect. Well, as perfect as you can.

Steps to the perfect marriage:

- **Go out on dates**. Set a time of the week where you can go to dinner and a movie. Get dressed up and act like you did when you first started dating. Hold hands, kiss, and cuddle. Once every six months or so try to take a romantic vacation in another town or state. Even if it is a simple date like renting a movie and turning off the phone that is a good way to get closer.

  "My husband and I started drifting apart. He would work then talk on the phone with his friends the rest of the night. Sometimes he would go to his friend's house and hang out. I am a stay at home mom and I don't have many good friends. I don't have time to just go out by myself. I also don't have people to watch my kids, when he offers to watch them I tell him that is a nice gesture but all I want to do is go out with him. One day I finally blew; I couldn't take him always ditching me so I told him that every night he has to turn off the phone and have one hour or more of together time. That is where we watch a movie, play a game, or watch TV together. We have to spend the whole hour straight together. It has made me a lot more happy with our relationship and I am more willing to be content with him talking on the phone or going to a friends house."

Beth, Age 26

- **Make him a "Honey To-do List".** If he is the type of guy that is lazy and makes you do everything for him, give him two things to do every day. You could make it once a week if they are big things. The things can be big or small but he has to get into the habit of helping you out around the house. I know too many women who have lazy husbands that expect the wife do everything. I'm not saying there aren't lazy women too. So this could be something you could do for your husband if you think you need to be more helpful around the house. Or even if you do everything this is something that will make things less overwhelming. Write down the two or three most important things that you want both of you to get done that day.

Example:
To do for me:
1) Do laundry
2) Clean floors
3) Go to the store

To do for him:
1) Fix broken drawer
2) Take out trash

- **Make him feel important.** Many of us are so conditioned to getting down on our husband's for small stuff they do wrong. We often take for granted that they are there at all. I'm not saying they are allowed to do anything to hurt us emotionally and get away with it. Choose your battles. If he forgets to do something on your "Honey To-Do List," don't flip out. Many times we inadvertently take out our anger on our husbands and kids. We get mad at them because someone was rude to us at the super market. Tell your husband at least once a day that you appreciate him. You will always get back the love and appreciation that you give out. Don't sit there expecting complements, live your life not expecting them, just because he doesn't say how much he needs you everyday doesn't mean he can live without you! It makes the moments he tells you all the more special.

How To Deal With You

◆

Part 12: Look Into Yourself

I know this book is mainly about how to deal with our mother-in-law. There is a ton of advice that hopefully you will take into consideration and help you feel better. After reading all that don't you feel a little better. I know I feel good about writing it. This part is about the most important person in any relationship, *you*. I would have put this part in the beginning of the book but I think it was therapeutic to have you read some horror/funny stories so you could blow off some steam and see that you are not alone in your struggle. Now you can feel better about going forward with you.

To help yourself you must build yourself with building blocks. All of the blocks are meant to help one another. There are three blocks I want to focus on, Mental, Spiritual, and Physical.

Mental:

The first of three important building blocks is our mental state. We need to be stronger within so we can deal with our surroundings a.k.a. mothers-in-law, sisters-in-law, brothers-in-law, fathers-in-law, women, or any other person you will come in contact with. Lets start off with a mental detox. **Forgetting the past**. The past doesn't even have to mean only the things that have long time passed. You will have to constantly, most likely every time you walk out her door have to forget what she does. I don't mean you totally have to forgive and forget because you will never truly forget. I mean try to focus on other things and not constantly remind yourself of the negative your mother-in-law brings.

Your mother-in-law might act worse towards you, your husband might act worse, but what if they get better? Are you going to be bitter and beat yourself up over it? She might give up one day and stop trying to take your husband. She will always love her son but may call less and know you have her beat. If you keep the hateful angry feelings you will be keeping all that negativity in your body and that will eat you up. You need to be a positive person.

> **Note**: Never let her repeat over and over bad things she does to you. If they get worse or have always been bad you have the right to stay away and forget her. Also if you keep reminding your husband of what your mother-in-law did years ago to the present, he will get sick of it and maybe it will ruin your marriage. Like I have said in a previous section, you need to blow off steam to someone else other then your husband. If you have no one then write it down.

Another way to forget is to **keep yourself busy**. If you have a lot of down time you will be reminding yourself of her. So get a hobby like making something and selling it or even just making things for your family. If you sell things it will help in two ways, you will have a hobby and you will feel you are contributing financially. You could make jewelry or put together photo albums. There are plenty of hobbies you could start learning. You could even take a class. You could go to a community college and take a cooking or an art class. They also have classes where you don't have to go to a college like painting or glass blowing. If you are a stay home mom like me things like this are very important to stay sane and converse with adults or just take time focusing on yourself. Even if you could get out once a week for a half an hour it would be good for you. I will talk about it more in the physical section but a great hobby would also be to go for walks or take a yoga class. It will help in multiple ways.

The next way to help out your mental well being is to **get rid of any insecurity**. Most women are very insecure including us. Isn't it funny when people are jealous of you when you don't think you are that great? I have a girlfriend who is 250 lbs. and women are very jealous of her because she is secure and has a great personality.

I have to admit I get jealous of girls if my husband looks at them. I get am enraged initially, but then after calming down I think to myself, "What am I doing? I am secure and happy with me." You have to build your self-esteem and be happy as *you*, to be happy with anything. *Only you can make yourself happy!*

I am not saying you have to be perfect. No one is, but be happy with everything you have. So in actuality you are perfect in your eyes. If you believe that others will too. Life will be much better for you all around.

Make a list of all the good things in your life. Write them on paper or type them on your computer. These are things that could be physical, such as your eyes, teeth, legs and so on. You can also write about everything you have accomplished in your life. The most important positive things you should write down that are non-physical would be your health and the health of your friends and family. There are so many people suffering everyday. We are so lucky to have what we do.

We are also very lucky we do not live in countries with wars going on. Where children don't mind if they blow you away. I have a good friend who came to stay with my husband and I this past weekend. He went to war in Iraq and saw so many people die. He said that he watched one of his friends get shot and killed by a little boy. He then had to kill the little boy because the boy was pointing his gun at him. How lucky are we that our children and we have it so well. We take these things for granted every day. Believe me all the things that you will be writing will over ride the negative things in your life by a million.

Meditation is very important in keeping a balanced and refreshed mental state. Find a quiet place like a closet or a bathroom. Then close your eyes and take deep breaths. Take time to clear your mind. Breathe in all the positive things surrounding you. Then exhale all the negative things in and around you. Do that for as long as you feel necessary it could be as long or as short as you want.

Spiritually:

Meditation important because if you believe in a higher power it would be a great time to get in touch with it. You can focus on telling them what you need help with in your life and ask for the strength to get it.

I do believe there is something more than this life. I think we are too amazing to just "die". I won't get too much into beliefs. I don't know the exact answers but I know just like our human nature that there is a good and an evil, a right and a wrong. So I strongly believe we should flock to the good or the positive so we can be positive people. That means as hard as it may seem we must give out positive to everyone including our mother-in-law. Remember positive breed's positive and negative breeds negative.

Physical:

Working out is very important to helping your all around happiness. When you work out you releases endorphins into your brain that actually make you feel happy. The easiest way to accomplish this endorphin release would be to walk. Try to walk a mile every other day if you can. Many people even walk around the mall. If you can, take a yoga class that would be another great way to exercise. Yoga would be good because it also allows you to meditate.

If you don't have much time you could do a short workout in your own house. But you have to try and do some kind of work out.

Losing weight. This is something that always seems to be on the minds of women. Too bad men aren't as concerned about it as we are. Men can let themselves go but women always have to be a certain weight in our society.

Don't ever feel that you have to be a twig to be beautiful. That's just not natural. If you start a diet pick one that looks the healthiest. Don't take pills or do the one-week fast. If you lose the weight too quickly you will gain it back even faster plus some. So start slow. Take everything one day at a time. Don't beat yourself up if you don't accomplish everything right away but know how rewarding it would be if you did accomplish it.

Fix yourself up once in a while. If you feel good looking nice then do it! But do it for you. It is always nice to have done your hair, put on makeup, and wear clothes that are a little dressier. I am so used to playing with my daughter and only wearing sweats and a T-shirt. Many times I won't do my hair or make up. When I do get the rare chance to take a shower fix my hair and do my make up I feel ten times better.

Pamper yourself. If you can save a little extra money for a day of pampering you should, even if it is just getting your nails done or getting a massage once a month. Doing this will help to relax you and you can believe with our lives we need it.

Conclusion

We unfortunately have to come to the end. I want to thank you again for reading this book. I hope and pray that you gained something from reading it. Whether it is comfort and strength in dealing with your in-laws, your husband, or even learned a little bit about yourself. I know I will need to read a few things over to myself to help me continue to "deal" with certain people. Hey, no one is perfect! I also hope you had a few laughs through reading these women's stories. Many of the women who told me their stories started to laugh after they told a horrific one. We all knew that despite the pain involved at the time of the incident, the things their mothers-in-law were doing were just plain ridiculous. That's how you are going to have to see it most of the time. That will help you out tremendously. Good-bye, good luck, and always stay positive in your journey!

0-595-32666-8

www.ingramcontent.com/pod-product-compliance
Lightning Source LLC
Chambersburg PA
CBHW020307290526
45784CB00003B/1397